Westminster Dragoons, first troops into Jerusalem 1917

THE YEOMANRY REGIMENTS

200 Years of Tradition

Patrick Mileham

Canongate Academic

For Alexandra, Felicity, Sally and Arabella

First published in 1985
200th Anniversary Edition
published in 1994 by
Canongate Academic
an imprint of Canongate Press Ltd
14 Frederick Street
Edinburgh EH2 2HB

ISBN 1 898410 36 4

British Library Cataloguing-in-Publication Data

A catalogue record for this book
is available on request from the
British Library

Printed and bound in Great Britain by
Butler & Tanner Ltd, Frome and London

Contents

Foreword

By The Marquess of Anglesey, FSA, FRHistS, FRSL, Hon, DLitt.

One of the best definitions of the word 'yeoman' is: 'a man free born'. Major Mileham's splendid book illustrates most comprehensively how over the last 190 years large numbers of yeomen have voluntarily agreed to forego part of their *personal* freedom so as to defend *national* freedom.

The military authorities and regular cavalry had an understandably ambivalent attitude towards the Yeomanry during the first half of its existence; its practical usefulness was never put to the test in battle. Latterly, in times of war, the military expertise of the yeomen and their steadiness in face of the enemy proved to be of the most reliable sort. Their response was entirely characteristic of their background.

It is a stirring story, one which would make no sense whatever to people who have never lived in a free society, but one which to the British reader will be a source of very real pride.

The Yeomanry Regiments is designed not only for those who are directly concerned with today's Yeomanry, such as former and serving members of regiments. It will also be, quite unquestionably, of the greatest interest to the general reader, for it is written in such a way as to conceal the enormous amount of erudition and research which lie behind its easy style.

Further, the military history of Britain has long suffered from the lack of a single volume devoted to this vitally important branch of the volunteer element of the land forces. There are numerous, detailed regimental histories, some good, more less so, written to very varying standards. Until now no-one has quarried in these and in other relevant works so as to produce one readable, concise chronicle. This glaring gap has now been filled comprehensively and extremely well, both verbally and pictorially.

Preface

By Colonel Sir Ralph Carr-Ellison, TD

In 1994 the Yeomanry is celebrating the two hundredth anniversary of its formation. Raised under threat of invasion from Revolutionary France, the Yeomanry Cavalry was formed amongst landowners and yeoman farmers who had a distinct position in British society, but were prompted by real patriotism and a determination to overcome the practical difficulties of raising and maintaining a large cavalry force.

As threat of invasion receded over the first hundred years, the Yeomanry took on the additional and perhaps unenviable task of rendering aid to the civil power. The Boer War in 1899–1902 saw a large number of Yeoman volunteers serving overseas for the first time. Mobilisation as complete regiments and active service in every theatre followed in the two World Wars. In the forty years of the Cold War, Yeomanry regiments prepared to fight either in North West Europe again or in home defence. Now in the 'capability based' rather than the 'threat based' British Army, the Yeomanry continues to train for new responsibilities with undiminished energy.

This book, in its first edition, fully captured the spirit of the Yeomanry, by displaying well-researched facts, with lively and descriptive writing and a set of brilliant illustrations. In his preface to the first edition, my distinguished predecessor, Colonel Sir Martin Gibbs, predicted confidently that the book 'will be well received by present and former yeomen and indeed by anyone who is concerned with the history of the Territorial Army'. He was right. We in the Yeomanry are all delighted that the author and publishers have produced a new and up-to-date edition to celebrate our bi-centenary.

Ralph Carr-Ellison

Author's Introduction

This illustrated history of the Yeomanry regiments is not intended to be a formal or exhaustive work on the subject. A definitive history is for another time. It is written for the non-specialist and tells, I hope vividly, the story of the Yeomanry from 1794 to the present. The illustrations, which evoke much of the spirit of these volunteer soldiers, show all aspects of service in the Yeomanry in peace and in war. The outline history and notes on the individual regiments which follow will, I trust, prove useful as a source of reference.

'Generalisations,' wrote Anatole France, 'are sometimes extremely serviceable.' In researching the subject, I met with more than the usual number of pitfalls for what, perhaps, should be a precisely regulated and well documented military organisation. Sources frequently conflict over detail; regimental and individual sensibilities abound; claims and counter-claims are put forward; denigration occasionally occurs; every regiment is 'second to none'.

Inevitably, therefore, I have had to be selective in making the story representative of the Yeomanry as a whole. No slight is intended to those regiments which are less well represented than others; and I hope that, on my part, I have not been too idiosyncratic. In defence I must state that I have been dealing with a highly idiosyncratic organisation, but I have tried to be as accurate and fair as possible in what I say about each regiment.

I have been assisted by a great number of knowledgeable, helpful, and interesting people. I must, in particular, thank the Marquess of Anglesey, the late Colonel Sir Martin Gibbs, Colonel Sir Ralph Carr-Ellison, Colonel J. E. B. Hills, Dr I. F. Beckett, Lieutenant-Colonel J. D. Sainsbury and W. Y. Carman Esq for their assistance and encouragement. Any failings or omissions in the book must, however, be ascribed not to them but to me. I should also like to thank the Museum Trusts, and a number of generous individuals who allowed me to use their photographs and who contributed to the sections on the regiments.

A second edition has allowed me to correct some errors and bring the history up to date. It has been a labour of love and I hope that readers will find it a useful introduction to a large, diverse and fascinating subject.

Gartmore
Stirlingshire

Patrick Mileham
April 1994

Part I
HISTORY OF THE YEOMANRY

1
The Threat of Invasion and the Raising of the Yeomanry Cavalry

Although William Pitt has long been credited with the raising of officially recognised volunteer corps for the defence of the Realm, the 1st Marquis Townshend had been involved in Parliamentary affairs in connexion with Militia reform since the 1750s. He had fought in the 1745 rebellion under Cumberland, took part in the continental campaigns during the Austrian War of Succession and served at the capture of Quebec. He raised the Norfolk Rangers in 1782, which were accepted as Yeomanry Cavalry in 1794, and was Colonel of the First or West Regiment of Norfolk Yeomanry Cavalry until his death in 1807.

– Suffolk and Norfolk Yeomanry

In February 1793 the French Revolutionary government declared war against Britain. During that year France became a 'nation under arms' under the direction of the dynamic Carnot, and when it was believed in early 1794 that the French intended to invade Britain, near panic ensued in London and the countryside.

The existing military forces were certainly insufficient to meet a determined invasion by the French. The Regular army was small and much of it was stationed overseas: six brigades were already fighting the French in the Netherlands alongside the Austrian army. The first line of reserve was the Militia which had been in existence in one form or another since the middle of the seventeenth century. By the late eighteenth century, it had developed into a form of conscripted service: each county was bound by Statute to raise men for the county Militia according to a quota fixed by the Government. Registers of men eligible for service were maintained and ballots were held to determine who was to serve. Substitutes could be provided but they had to be paid by the individuals for whom they were standing substitute. Troops of Militia Horse existed in some parts of the country.

Militia regiments were embodied for permanent duty, sometimes for many months, and Militia service was universally unpopular. Many of the rank and file were of the disreputable strata of society, and in relation to its cost, the Militia was of very uncertain effectiveness in times of danger. Drastic reforms of the Force,

Westminster Cavalry 1798, by Rowlandson.

– Westminster Dragoons

designed to improve its efficiency and reliability, would not have been possible to achieve swiftly or cheaply.

In times of national danger in the past, volunteer corps had often been formed and these had included cavalry troops: but as they had mainly been raised unofficially they were usually short-lived. In some parts 'Fencible' regiments were employed, both of infantry and cavalry, which comprised full-time volunteers who were recruited for the duration of a war for home service.

From the time of the Civil War in the mid-seventeenth century there had been close Parliamentary and later Ministerial control of the Army and the Militia. Now it was seen that the acceptance of voluntary military service could be encouraged and regulated for the more effective defence of the realm in the event of invasion. By statutory and administrative measures, first used during the American War of Independence, volunteers could be embodied and control exercised over them by the granting of commissions to volunteer officers, by providing their weapons and voting for their pay.

There was also in 1794 much fear in Britain that a landing by the French Citizen Army would be welcomed by certain factions who had rejoiced in the success of the French Revolution. The disaffection caused by rural poverty and the Industrial Revolution was strong in many parts of the country. The British Jacobins, however, proved well versed in rhetoric but they were lacking in overall direction, so that the threat from inside the country, although a very real one, was localised and uncoordinated.

In the face of this threat the British government, led by the Younger Pitt, decided to increase the Militia and, in addition, to capitalise on the willingness of volunteer soldiers to serve as enrolled corps. A bill was first read on 27 March 1794 for 'encouraging and disciplining such Corps and companies of men, as shall voluntarily enrol themselves for the Defence of their counties, towns or coasts, or for the General defence of the Kingdom, during the present war'. Since the formation of volunteer cavalry in large numbers was deemed essential, the Bill was swiftly passed, and this mounted arm became generally known as the 'Gentlemen and Yeomanry Cavalry'. The word 'yeoman' came from Middle English, and meant a freeholder under the rank of Gentleman and of respectable standing.

When called out by the Lord Lieutenant or High Sheriff the volunteer soldiers were to be embodied and made ready to defend their own or neighbouring counties in the event of invasion. (Some corps voted for service anywhere in the country.) Public meetings of patriotic and influential people were held all over the country for the formation and support of the Yeomanry and Volunteer corps.

Over the years many Acts of Parliament were to follow, regulating and modifying the Militia, Yeomanry and Volunteers. The purpose was to improve their efficiency and usefulness whilst maintaining their cost at the lowest possible level.

Commissions were granted on the King's authority by the Lords Lieutenant, although lists of names were subject to ministerial scrutiny. Officer appointments were held by the nobility and gentry whilst the ranks were filled by landholders and tenant farmers. The men had to provide their own mounts: saddlery and uniforms were to be paid for by the officers or by subscriptions raised in the counties. In due course their arms – curved swords with simple hilts, horse pistols and a proportion of carbines – were to be provided by the Government. Members of the Yeomanry were exempted from the Militia ballot as long as they attended a

A corporal of an Ayrshire Yeomanry Corps in 1798. A modern artist's reconstruction by Douglas Anderson.

– Ayrshire Yeomanry

required number of days' training. Each member was paid for embodied service and subject to military law in the event of invasion, or to dismissal for infringement of discipline at other times. Strict regulations were also issued by the Home Office concerning the responsibilities of Lords Lieutenant and Commanding Officers, periodic strength returns, certification of embodied service and issues of arms, and permission for permanent duty.

In their early days the Yeomanry corps paraded frequently. As the danger from abroad decreased, so the frequency of their training tended to decline. Since most of the yeomen were farmers they were obviously keen that their military duties should not interfere with their work on the land. Later on the requirement for parading, especially annual 'permanent duty', was more closely regulated.

The Yeomanry Cavalry was an exclusive and prestigious organisation. Membership undoubtedly enhanced the social standing of those who joined its ranks, and enabled them to escape the stigma of service in the ranks of the Militia. The aristocratic and land-owning tradition of the Yeomanry persisted very strongly in some areas until quite recent times. For many county families voluntary military service was a matter of course for successive generations, maintaining the exclusiveness of the Yeomanry until the wars of the twentieth century altered the pattern and requirements of service.

The circumstances that led to embodiment for duty, apart from the threat of invasion, included 'the suppression of riots and tumults' when the Yeomanry could be called out to assist the Civil power. In this respect there was both an instinctive and deliberate purpose which united members of the Yeomanry, binding together those whose interest lay in the preservation of the monarchy, the Constitution and private property.

In the first year, 1794, 28 corps or troops of Yeomanry were raised. Some corps from the start identified themselves with a county regimental title and unified command. But the greatest strength of the Yeomanry lay in the troop which numbered anything up to 60 strong.

The government, however, was not satisfied that there were sufficient volunteer cavalrymen, and so the Provisional Cavalry Act was passed in 1796. This required every person who owned ten or more horses to provide one fully equipped horseman for service in the Provisional Cavalry. It was a highly unpopular measure, but it caused local committees to raise additional Yeomanry corps. Records show that 31 new corps were raised that year; and by 1799, 206 troops were listed.

By the time of the Peace of Amiens, which temporarily brought a halt to hostilities in 1802, most English counties, many Welsh and some Scottish counties boasted anything from one to twenty or more troops of Yeomanry, centred around towns, villages and estates. For example, in Lancashire in 1797, troops were formed in Manchester, Liverpool, Salford and Bolton. The following year the Blackburn and Oldham troops were added and, in 1800, the Bury troop. Two more troops were raised later in Furness and Wigan. Frequently troops were to be found centred on the landed estates of noblemen and gentlemen, such as the Badminton troop, the Dalemain troop, Woodstock troop, Parham troop, Holkham troop, Eaton troop, Cobham (Kent) troop, Chudleigh troop and many more. Some were named after their noble commanding officers. In London there were a number of mounted corps such as the Westminster Cavalry and the Loyal Islington Troop.

In Ireland, too, many corps of cavalry were formed at this time. Their membership tended to fluctuate dramatically and they inevitably represented the Protestant Ascendancy.

Throughout the Revolutionary and Napoleonic wars, there were many rumours of invasion. Beacons were often lit in panic and cattle made ready to be driven to safety inland. The Yeomanry and Volunteers frequently assembled. There was one notable occasion in the Lowlands of Scotland in January 1804 when more than 3,000 volunteers, including the various Yeomanry corps, turned out to face what was long remembered as the 'False Alarm'.

In 1797, however, there had been a landing by 1400 French soldiers in Pembrokeshire, although any real danger to the country as a whole was much less than the fear it engendered. This was one of three expeditionary enterprises. The largest, numbering 15,000, was supposed to land in Bantry Bay in Ireland, while a third small force had the purpose of a raid on Newcastle. The French assumed that Britain was so close to a state of revolution that they could 'march on London with wooden swords' at the head of an English mob.

The force which appeared off the Pembroke coast on 22 February 1797 was meant to raid Bristol. It was commanded by General Tate (an American of Irish extraction), and the ships were sailing under false British colours. That evening the force landed, together with large supplies of ammunition; but the troops were not provisioned with food since they were expected to live off the land. A high proportion of them were convicts from the gaols and many were actually British nationals. Once ashore the force was dismayed to see their ships set sail.

This primitive painting by an unknown Welsh artist depicts the surrender of the French at Goodwick Sands near Fishguard in 1797. The Castlemartin Yeomanry can be seen in the foreground.

– Carmarthenshire Antiquarian Society/Dyfed County Council

On hearing the news – and the false colours had not fooled the local people – the whole country was in a fever of activity. Lord Milford appointed Lord Cawdor, who commanded the Castlemartin Yeomanry, to command the volunteer forces which gathered between the invaders and Fishguard during 23 February. The country people also assembled, bearing whatever arms could be found or fashioned. Even the lead was stripped off the roof of St David's Cathedral for shot: it was explained to the indignant clergy that the Church as well as the State had to be defended.

The French, however, did not form for battle; instead they set off in small parties in search of food. Indeed apart from a few skirmishes involving small numbers only, the hapless French had no stomach for a fight and soon signalled their intention to surrender. Under the watchful eyes of the Castlemartin Yeomanry, Militia, Fencibles, armed sailors and a huge crowd of local people, the invaders marched to Goodwick Sands and laid down their arms.

In 1802, after the Peace of Amiens, the Yeomanry Cavalry were thanked for their services and given the option of disbandment, which most corps declined to accept. A year later, when war was resumed, the Yeomanry Cavalry was increased in size to about 36,000 officers and men. The government also urged the regimenting of troops for greater control and efficiency, but many troops remained independent for years.

Command and control of the various volunteer military corps in each county were mostly haphazard. The efficiency and effectiveness of the Yeomanry depended on the energy of the officers and men and the strength of local ties.

Indeed even regular regiments on home duty were not controlled in a way that would be recognisable today. The Lord Lieutenant of the county was responsible to the monarch, and the volunteer commanding officers were answerable to the Lord Lieutenant. Control of the volunteers was exercised by the Home Secretary until 1871, when it passed to the Secretary of State for War.

Military formality and concerted action were very much dependent on the co-operation and good sense of the officers. When regiments were 'brigaded' the senior commanding officer assumed temporary command. Despite these limitations, in many parts of the country comprehensive contingency plans were drawn up, coasts were watched, signal-beacons were made ready, military manoeuvres held, supplies organised after a fashion, and arms and accoutrements issued – all in a spirit of great enthusiasm as well as a natural and very real fear of invasion from France. The Yeomanry paraded frequently, mustered for 'permanent duty', practised their horsemanship, drills and manoeuvres, tried to accustom their horses to the sound of gunfire, and maintained their arms and equipment to a reasonable standard of serviceability.

A yeoman of the Pembroke (Castlemartin) Yeomanry Cavalry 1803. He wears a Tarleton helmet, common to most Yeomanry Cavalry Corps of the time and carries a sword and flintlock pistol. A modern artist's reconstruction, by Lt Col Olaf MacLeod.

– Pembroke Yeomanry

Despite the later cessation of hostilities after the battle of Waterloo in 1815, the Yeomanry Cavalry was much in demand for service in aid of the Civil Power and some new corps were raised specifically for this purpose. But the vagaries of the government's policy and its unwillingness to pay for military service resulted in further disbandments in 1827–8. Twenty-two corps, (comprising 144 troops) were authorised to continue officially. A further sixteen corps, of 66 troops, were accepted without pay. Thus the strength of the Yeomanry was reduced by two-thirds, the criteria for official retention being based on the frequency of individual corps being called out in aid of the Civil Power during the previous ten years. Three years later, however, the government called for the re-raising of many corps in view of the dangerous state of the country, and the total strength was doubled. In 1838 reductions took place once again – the start of a cycle which persists to the present day.

'Village Cavalry practising in a Farmyard.' A contemporary cartoon by Rowlandson.

– Inns of Court and City Yeomanry

2

'Riots and Tumults': the Yeomanry and Military Aid to the Civil Power

'The Peterloo Massacre' – This contemporary print shows the Manchester and Cheshire Yeomanry Cavalry charging the crowd in St Peter's Field, Manchester on 17 August 1819. The sympathy of the artist is unmistakably with the Radicals and he has chosen not to show regular cavalrymen who took as much a part as the yeomen.

– The Mansell Collection

In Britain during the nineteenth century regular troops and the Militia were frequently used to prevent rioting, disperse mobs and provide guards and escorts. Before the establishment of police forces the magistrates were often forced to call upon the military. From the early days of the Yeomanry the civil authorities began to rely on it as an effective force for preventing and quelling disturbances.

By 1793 Thomas Paine's *The Rights of Man* had sold 200,000 copies. In the following year so many seditious meetings were held up and down the country that Habeas Corpus was suspended. Frequent demands for the improvement of conditions and the lowering of the basic food prices were made both in the countryside and the towns. Later, demands for Constitutional and Parliamentary reform created situations of tension and widespread violence.

In 1795 there were riots all over the country. One of the many instances took place in Devon when Sir Stafford Northcote's volunteer Troop of Cavalry was despatched to Crediton to assist the 25th Light Dragoons to restore order and make arrests. In the same county, in 1816, a mob forced entry into Bideford prison in order to release their detained ringleaders. Members of various troops of the North Devon Yeomanry assembled quickly and, led by four officers, patrolled the town all night; several rioters were arrested and escorted to Exeter.

Some of the urban corps were disliked by the working class, as much for their parvenu background as for their effectiveness at controlling the disturbances. In 1819 the Yeomanry were involved in what became the most famous incident of the military attempting to control civil disturbance, the 'Peterloo Massacre' in Peter's Field, Manchester, where a crowd of 60,000 was assembled. When the meeting got out of hand, the crowd stampeded to get away from the regular and volunteer troops who had been ordered to make arrests. Eleven people were killed and over five hundred were injured. There were two immediate results – a surge in recruiting for the Yeomanry and an increase in the vilification of the Yeomanry by those whose political sympathies lay with the Manchester crowd. Thus a few months later, in their county town, members of the Warwickshire Yeomanry were taunted and set upon by a mob calling them 'Manchester butchers who cut up women and children!'

In many parts of the country at this time the danger to the government was indeed great. The Radical movement had spread and there were attempts to foment strikes and armed rebellion in order to force constitutional change. In particular there was 'A state of excitement in Scotland' in early 1820 which affected the manufacturing areas. 60,000 operatives did in fact strike against work, but only a handful took to armed resistance against the forces of the Crown, which included regular troops, Volunteers and Yeomanry numbering altogether about 3,000 men. The non-regular troops were called out on 2 April, and, on 5 April members of the Kilsyth troop of the Stirlingshire Yeomanry Cavalry, together with some members of the 10th Hussars, pursued a band of armed rebels. Showing a good deal of courage the rebels fired shots and faced a charge of the King's men at Bonnymuir near Falkirk. There were no fatalities, but eighteen of the Radicals were arrested, and two were later convicted of High Treason and hanged. The encounter was thereafter called the 'Battle of Bonnymuir'.

The Staffordshire Yeomanry was probably involved in more incidents than any

This watercolour impression of the Wiltshire Yeomanry Cavalry shows them facing a mob at the so called 'Battle of Pythouse' in 1830. The anxiety of the yeomen must have been deeper and longer lasting in connexion with agrarian trouble when compared with the more immediate physical danger of facing urban rioters. Instances of intimidation and seizure of weapons from the homes of yeomen are recorded.

– Royal Wiltshire Yeomanry

This print shows The Seventh Duke of Beaufort Commanding the Royal Gloucestershire Yeomanry Cavalry c1840. The officers wore a curious type of shako during this period.

– Royal Gloucestershire Hussars

other corps. In 1822 Staffordshire 'Colliers who refused to work were determined to prevent others from doing so, maltreating them and ducking them, even to the very point of drowning. The Bilston Troop was sent for to protect the working colliers and to disperse the mob, which was done, but not without some resistance being made as a few shots were fired and a rioter was mortally wounded'.

Widespread and serious trouble occured during the 1830s. For instance, the Hindon Troop of the Wiltshire Yeomanry faced 500 rioters in Tisbury in 1830. In the same year in other places in the county, the Wiltshire Yeomanry had to round up gangs intent on destroying farm machinery. The following year the Dodington and Tetbury troops were sent to Bristol to work with two regular cavalry regiments in quelling a highly dangerous disturbance when the Bishop's Palace and other public buildings were burnt to the ground by a mob. There were also serious riots in South Wales and a troop of the Swansea Cavalry was met by a crowd which, appearing to be peaceful, first engulfed the yeomen and then disarmed them. It was a carefully planned ruse.

Chartist riots in the period 1837–42 frequently necessitated the use of the Yeomanry. In 1839 Monmouth was attacked by Welsh miners, some of whom carried firearms, while elsewhere there was evidence of preparation for revolutionary action. From small towns – such as Llanidloes where in 1839 the Chartists held the town for five days and the Montgomeryshire Yeomanry had to appear in force – to the major centres of population such as Birmingham, Nottingham, Manchester, Chester, Derby, Leeds, Stoke-on-Trent, Bolton and London – the Yeomanry was regularly involved in helping to keep the peace in this period.

Escorts were frequently called upon to guard royalty or officers of the law or indeed prisoners. One such gruesome task, which the Appleby troop had to undertake, was when a seventeen-year-old youth was led to his public execution outside Carlisle in 1829. As late as 1845 the Mayor of Chipping Norton wrote urgently to the Lord Lieutenant asking for a troop of the Oxfordshire Hussars for the following day to protect the town from 'serious riot and probably bloodshed' after a police constable had apprehended a man 'and whose death it had been assumed by the mob ensued from violence by the Constable'.

In 1832 the same regiment had been put on permanent duty in the area of Otmoor to 'aid and assist the Civil Power in the preservation of Peace and protection of property'. Land enclosure had been the grievance. 'Fifty-seven rioters were arrested and taken by a troop of twenty-one yeomen to Oxford, but on entering the city, the escort was set upon by a mob of over a thousand strong, armed with stones, sticks and brickbats, which they hurled at the Yeomanry. In the confusion the prisoners quickly escaped, but were subsequently recaptured.' Great restraint was shown, it was recorded, by the yeomen 'in repelling the

This engraving shows two forms of dress worn by Officers of the South Salopian Yeomanry Cavalry, c1830.

– Shropshire Yeomanry

Officers of the Glasgow and Lower Ward of Lanarkshire Yeomanry Cavalry c1853.

– National Army Museum

A non-commissioned officer of the Westmorland and Cumberland Yeomanry c1847. Engraving after a painting by R. Harrington.

– R. Hasell McCosh Esq

assaults and insults of the mob without using their firearms'. Valour seems to have been a necessary part of discretion on such occasions.

In 1846 the Westmorland and Cumberland Yeomanry were called out to prevent pitched battles between English and Irish navvies working on the Carlisle to Lancaster railway when the town of Penrith was threatened.

The unpopularity of the Yeomanry in some areas provided evidence of its effectiveness in aiding the Civil Power. The existence of volunteer mounted troops with local knowledge, able to assemble and disperse quickly, helped to decrease the level of organised and spontaneous violence in Britain during the first half of the nineteenth century. During this period they were often the only reliable and effective force for public order other than the Regular Army. In some places, however, the use of Yeomanry was deliberately avoided, because its appearance had tended to exacerbate the situation on previous occasions, rather than contribute to the maintenance of order.

The establishment of effective police forces (by 1829 in London and 1855 in the counties) resulted, however, in a diminishing requirement for the Yeomanry to be called out; and the last occasion on which the magistrates called for assistance from the Yeomanry was during food riots in Devon in 1867. A detachment of 112 officers and men of the Royal 1st Devon Yeomanry paraded in Exeter, and their presence was enough to contain the level of violence.

3
Yeomanry Service in the Nineteenth Century

Many Yeomanry regiments continued to serve after the need for them to help maintain law and order diminished. New fears of invasion in 1848, 1851 and 1859, during the period of French expansionism under Napoleon III, re-emphasised the importance of maintaining adequate forces for home defence. A number of new mounted corps were raised, Light Horse and Mounted Rifles as well as Yeomanry. There were precise differences between these types of corps in terms of commitment to serve, but individual units themselves often caused the distinctions to become obscured.

Light Horse volunteers differed from the Yeomanry Cavalry regiments in their constitution and terms of service. They were normally raised in the large cities and had no commitment for service other than for the defence of their immediate locality. Some 'Light Horse' corps, however, were accepted for service on the same terms as the Yeomanry Cavalry according to the various statutes and regulations governing such matters. The name 'Volunteer Cavalry' was more popular amongst the urban corps than 'Yeomanry Cavalry' with its rural or provincial connotations.

The Yeomanry were deemed to be light or auxiliary cavalry. Some adopted the titles of Hussars and Dragoons in the early years whilst others adopted the name of Lancers later in the nineteenth century. At first they were armed with sword and pistol, but increasingly they came to be issued with rifled carbines and were transformed, in effect, into riflemen.

This finally resulted in a mounted force which met the requirement expressed as early as 1798 by General John Money. This redoubtable soldier – a veteran of the Seven Years' War, the American War and the French Revolutionary war who later commanded the 3rd Regiment of Norfolk Yeomanry – had challenged the usefulness of cavalry in Britain which could neither fight dismounted nor form properly to charge an enemy. The nature of the British countryside, he pointed out, was scarcely suitable for 'continental' cavalry tactics which required great expanses of open space.

If the Yeomanry officers ever entertained the idea that they could emulate the famous continental cavalry actions on British soil, they were not given the opportunity. Cavalry formations and manoeuvres at speed require great skill, concentration, discipline and practice. At first many of the manoeuvres were carried out at the halt, although later the Yeomanry were to achieve much greater proficiency. There was always a shortage of mounts for the Dragoon and Dragoon Guard regiments and the Yeomanry used ordinary riding horses or hunters, which were the men's own property.

They considered that the sword was their true weapon, and great importance

Thomas Potter MacQueen Esq MP is depicted in this engraving as a Lieutenant Colonel of the Bedfordshire Yeomanry Cavalry in 1864.

– National Army Museum

Dismounted swordsmen competing for prizes in May 1850. This scene shows members of the Montgomeryshire Yeomanry Cavalry at Victoria Bowling Green, Welshpool. Engraving by C. Hutchins of Liverpool.

– Powysland Museum, Welshpool

was therefore placed on swordsmanship. Standard regular cavalry drills were adopted over the years, and the cavalry sword developed from the rudimentary curved cutting weapon to straighter patterns of more serviceable design and better balance.

The political power and influence of the Yeomanry and Volunteers was always considerable. One regiment, the Queen's Own West Kent Yeomanry, boasted two members of the Upper House and six members of the Commons serving at one time in the 1880s. This was by no means exceptional, and such political representation ensured that the interests of the volunteers were powerfully supported.

The nineteenth century was the period par excellence for the proliferation and extravagance of uniforms. Commanding officers received only small allowances

A number of Yeomanry Cavalry regiments contained integral infantry sections. This rare photograph shows Wiltshire yeomen and the curious conveyance which was probably specially designed and built for them.

– Royal Wiltshire Yeomanry

for uniforms and the money had to be found by the officers, local committees and the men themselves. They naturally tended to choose colourful and flamboyant garb. In the early years tailed jackets, white breeches, boots and leather helmets, were adopted. The shako, at first bell-topped, bedecked with hair or feather plumes, came to be worn. Trousers of various cut replaced breeches. Later in the century regiments tended to adopt either Hussar or Dragoon uniforms, the former consisting of busbies and short jackets with silver lace and braid ornamentation; and the latter fuller jackets of a simpler design and the metal or leather 'Albert' helmet. Various forms of undress uniforms were adopted, while the magnificent full dress (for Hussars complete with pelisse) was worn for musters and field days as well as formal parades, reviews and levees.

This engraving shows the East and West Regiments of Kent Yeomanry Cavalry at Mote Park, Maidstone. Lord Romney, the Lord Lieutenant of Kent entertained both Regiments on the grand occasion of the Review in 1837.

– Kent and Sharpshooters Yeomanry

The Yeomanry also knew how to entertain themselves, particularly once the country had become more tranquil. In early days there had been few barracks even for regular troops, and since it was necessary to billet the Yeomanry in hotels and public houses, there was often much drinking and merriment. When assembled for permanent duty, dinners and balls for the yeomen as well as officers were frequently held. Naturally racing was a favourite pastime.

When the Yeomanry formed for Field Days, Reviews, evolutions or 'permanent duty', often the most lavish entertainment was laid on for them. Thus in 1837 Lord Romney entertained the East and West Kent Yeomanry Cavalry, numbering about seven hundred at Mote Park. Between drills and races the troops consumed a meal 'of the most sumptuous description, and the tables groaned under substantial old English fare'. A second sitting enabled his lordship's 'peasantry and their families to partake of the inviting viands, and also some fine old English ale'. The 'necessitous poor' received the remainder. A great number of notable people witnessed the festivities which must have been the greatest occasion in the county that year.

As the future of mounted troops seemed secure the Yeomanry continued to train in their traditional cavalry role; but increasingly they paid attention to mounted reconnaissance, flank protection and picquets – tasks which previous generations of cavalrymen had considered to be beneath their dignity. Later on musketry became very popular, encouraged by the Rifle Volunteer movement in the 1860s, and competitions and meetings were held regularly.

An NCO of the Fife Light Horse is shown displaying the practice of tent pegging during training in 1898.

– Sir John Gilmour Bart

This elegant print shows members of the Cheshire Yeomanry at mounted sword practice c1890.

– Cheshire Yeomanry

Royal North Devon Hussars on Parade at the funeral of their Honorary Colonel Sir Arthur Chichester at Shirwell 1898.

– Royal Devon Yeomanry

OUR YEOMANRY
'Didn't you hear the order to dismount?'
'Yes, Zur.'
'Then why didn't you dismount?'
'Becos if I did, Zur, I couldn't git hup agin.'

– A contemporary cartoon in the possession of the Kent and Sharpshooters Yeomanry

The second half of the nineteenth century witnessed both the rise of the Rifle Volunteer movement and the Cardwell reforms. The establishing of efficient infantry battalions of enthusiastic volunteers, and radical changes in the organisation of reserve forces in conjunction with the Regular Army, paved the way for the Territorial Force and Territorial Army of the present century. The organisation and training of the Yeomanry underwent many changes, often as a result of the formal work of commissions of enquiry and legislation. For instance in 1888 the Yeomanry became liable for service anywhere in the country in the event of invasion.

Yeomanry regiments were brigaded according to district and the squadron became the normal sub-unit. 'Permanent duty' was conducted each year, increasingly based on tented camps, and these periods of camp were chosen to avoid seeding, haymaking and harvesting as far as possible. Periodic parade and training inspections were carried out by officers from the regular cavalry. Training of individuals was conducted throughout the year, and the pattern of volunteer service became much as it is for the present-day Territorial Army – but of course lacking the pace and intensity of modern-day soldiering.

4
The Boer War: the Imperial Yeomanry

Since its inception it had never been intended that the Yeomanry should serve overseas; indeed it was prevented from service abroad by Statute. This was to change, however, as a result of the extraordinary events of the colonial war in South Africa, which necessitated providing a very large number of troops in what swiftly became a major war.

The closing months of 1899 were disastrous for the British army in South Africa. The Boers had attacked across the Natal border and westwards into the Transvaal. Three British counter-strokes against the invaders at Stormberg, Magersfontein and Colenso failed in one single week in December – 'Black Week'. There was consternation at home: regular British troops were suffering

This camp is probably Maitland Camp near Cape Town. Many battalions of the Imperial Yeomanry passed through here after landing in South Africa, and this photograph depicts the horse lines of the Middlesex Yeomanry of the 34th and 35th Companies.

– Suffolk & Norfolk Yeomanry

heavy casualties and defeat at the hands of irregular Boer forces.

The Boers' success was due particularly to their accurate small-arms shooting at extreme ranges and the unorthodox tactics they adopted in the vast open countryside. The Boer farmers, mounted on hardy horses, fought with determined ferocity and, as long as they could maintain the initiative, were able to strike with great speed. A small number of Boers could thus cause havoc amongst very much larger and better equipped regular soldiers by forcing them to dissipate their strength over wide areas of country. The Boers used artillery for laying siege on some of the British garrisons, but usually they fought in mounted columns called commandos. Just as the regulars had suffered, so were the volunteers from Britain and the Dominions to suffer the difficulties of fighting the enemy on equal terms. Indeed it was only overwhelming numbers, and the starving of the Boers of supplies, which eventually resulted in their seeking peace.

On 18 December 1899 the British government appealed for volunteers. Special legislation was passed enabling volunteer soldiers to be used outside Britain in specially formed volunteer units. The response was remarkable. Meetings were held up and down the country reminiscent of the time a hundred years earlier when Britain was threatened by revolutionary France. Companies of 'Imperial Yeomanry' (IY) were formed, the Yeomanry regiments thus providing the nucleus for one or more companies.

A number of completely new units were formed from volunteers who could ride well and were keen shots. The companies were formed loosely into battalions of Imperial Yeomanry which, from the start, were expected to fight in the mounted rifle role. They were armed with Enfield rifles, while many of the battalions contained Colt or Maxim gun sections.

Within weeks the battalions of Imperial Yeomanry were embarked and sailing for South Africa. The sea voyage in hastily adapted ships had first to be experienced, and as was usual on sea voyages, many of the horses did not survive. The provision of horses for the war was a major task for the Army Remount Service, which had to acquire over 400,000 horses from all over the world. A high proportion of them proved to be of barely acceptable quality.

On landing, the troops concentrated in various camps and entrained for journeys of hundreds of miles into the interior. 'Keen, eager, full of energy and enthusiastic,' a war correspondent wrote, 'they are also most resourceful and

This photograph shows the 43rd (Suffolk) Company IY on their arrival in South Africa in early 1900. They do not appear to have been issued with rifle buckets since their rifles are slung awkwardly on their backs.

– Suffolk and Norfolk Yeomanry

ingenious in adapting their knowledge of country life to the conditions found in the veldt.' But this was a matter of survival and both regular and volunteer soldiers had to learn quickly some very hard lessons. For this had proved to be a war of no fixed front, of sieges and the relief of sieges, of long marches, patrolling, reconnaissance, flank guards, and the guarding of supply columns, as well as driving away cattle, clearing Boer settlements, fighting the elusive Boer commandos and seeking to dominate the veldt and hold the towns.

There were many notable engagements during the ensuing two years in which the companies of Imperial Yeomanry were involved. In May 1900 the 23 (Duke of Lancaster's Own) Company and 24 (Westmorland and Cumberland) Company of the 8th Battalion were surprised at Faber Putts in a dawn attack. They sustained many casualties but managed to beat off the Boers. In the following month Piet De Wet, one of the most successful Boer Commanders and brother of Christian, surrounded a column of Yeomanry at Lindley in the Orange River Colony and forced them to surrender. The effect of this fiasco was to raise doubts at home concerning the wisdom of employing enthusiastic but relatively untrained volunteers in a type of warfare that demanded experienced soldiers and expert leadership. Soon afterwards, however, the 17 (Ayrshire) Company conducted one of the most brilliant night marches of the war in appalling conditions to relieve Potchefstroom, the old capital of the Transvaal.

On one occasion the Boers of Commandant Wessel's column carried out a bold ruse on a British column which included the Pembrokeshire and Montgomeryshire companies. The yeomen came up against five groups each of about one hundred khaki-clad horsemen in close formation. Assuming them to be yeomen from another British column, they were allowed to approach close by: a desperate battle followed, some guns were captured and there were many casualties on each side. The Pembroke and Montgomery yeomen put in a charge and managed to retrieve the guns; Private Jones of Pembroke was decorated with the DCM for a valiant and dangerous ride to contact the other British column in the same area.

On another occasion a Cheshire Company was part of a force that was pursuing

Men of 22nd (Cheshire) Company IY man a 'sconce' overlooking Koegas Pont, a ferry on the River Koegas. The company spent some months on this task as did many other companies on similar static duties.

– Cheshire Yeomanry

The first action of the 4th Battalion IY on 26 April 1900 at Wakkerstroom. The CO, Colonel Blair and Bn HQ staff watch the action which was many hundreds of yards distance.

– Staffordshire Yeomanry/ Major T. H. Gardner

Lord Lovat, who raised the Lovat Scouts, is seen here on the right in an off-duty moment in South Africa. It cannot be denied that vestiges of feudal enthusiasm attended such men in raising volunteer units for service in the Boer War.

– Lovat Scouts

Christian De Wet which was thwarted only by his lucky escape during a fearful storm. On Good Friday 1901 the same company galloped in darkness to fight off a Boer attack on Koegas Pont, a vital bridge over the Orange River. Indeed it was the impassability on many stretches of the rivers in bad weather which dictated the movements of the Boer commandos and, in particular, their supplies and artillery.

In May 1901, 48 (North Somerset) Company, working with the two Devon companies as the rearguard of General Dixon's column, was ambushed. On one side of the route was a rough hillside, on the other long veldt grass in which a gunpowder trail had been laid. The Boers charged, shouting that they were the Scottish Horse. The rearguard was soon surrounded but refused to surrender. The smoke and burning grass added to the plight of the soldiers; some of the wounded were burnt to death. 60 out of 150 yeomen were killed before relief arrived.

41st Company of the Hampshire Carabiniers are seen here observing from the top of a ridge. Captain Seeley (who later commanded the Regiment) has the spy-glass; most yeomen possessed field-glasses, very often purchased at their own expense.

– Staffordshire Yeomanry/ Major T. H. Gardner

This photograph shows members of the 2nd Battalion Imperial Yeomanry watering horses.

– Cheshire Yeomanry

The inscription on this curious mule-drawn vehicle is 'Galloping Ambulance, 43rd Company IY.' In the possession of the Suffolk Yeomanry are earlier photographs of this regimental Medical NCO, who was clearly a great character and of somewhat advanced age for active service.

– Suffolk and Norfolk Yeomanry

One of the new regiments of Imperial Yeomanry, the 2nd Scottish Horse, showed great determination in guarding a column on trek west of Pretoria. At Vlakfontein, Lieutenant English was awarded the Victoria Cross for successfully repulsing an attack by a Boer force three times the strength of his troop. Later an attack on a section of the column was fiercely resisted. The enemy strength was seven times as great and only six out of 79 of the Scottish Horse remained unwounded; many were killed. Lord Tullibardine, who had raised the two regiments from South African Scots and from the home country, himself succeeded in raiding a Boer remount farm and fighting off his pursuers for many miles.

These yeomen of the 4th Battalion IY have dismounted in dead ground in order to approach a kopje which they probably considered clear of enemy. To have appeared on top of it mounted could have been spotted by the enemy from a great distance.

– Staffordshire Yeomanry/ Major T. H. Gardner

For a period one company, made up of Dorset, Devon and Sussex yeomen, joined with two squadrons of Rough Riders and one of the Fife Light Horse, under the overall command of Colonel Colvin of the Rough Riders. The column had the task of clearing an area in the Transvaal, and there was stiff fighting to capture some high ground dominating the Boer town of Parys. The town was then entered but it proved to be a major task to follow the Boers who were leaving with their families and possessions and firing at the British as they went. It was often as dangerous to follow the Boers as to allow them to escape.

In the incident some Boer waggons, whose horses had bolted, gave the yeomen 'as good as a run with the East Fife Hounds, and then Tally Ho for the next ridge'. But at the next ridge the yeomen were fired on by a party of fifty Boers, part of a group of 300–500 strong. It was fortunate that the Boers withdrew since the Yeomanry force was only 40 strong.

During the two years of the Boer War many additional companies of Yeomanry were formed, some of them on a regional basis, which subsequently formed the nucleus of the eighteen 'new' county regiments of Imperial Yeomanry at home. Throughout 1900 and the early part of 1901 new drafts of Yeomanry from Britain and new mounts from South America arrived in South Africa. Some of the 'old' companies were replaced by 'new' companies bearing the same titles. Kitchener's programme of block-house building along the extensive lines of communications and starving the Boers of supplies until they became reckless, gradually reduced the Boers' forces. During 1901 several of the Yeomanry and volunteer units were sent home, their job having been done. Many yeomen had lost their lives, thousands had been wounded or suffered enteric fever, but the IY had acquitted itself well. 'The care of their horses was a beautiful sight,' a correspondent wrote, and experience of active warfare made them 'less reckless and more cautious . . . and all the while full of an earnest desire for a fight.' 'South Africa' was to be the first battle honour of the twentieth century and it was worn proudly on the guidons of the Yeomanry regiments.

The Hertfordshire Yeomanry at Stables during Annual Camp Berkhampstead 1901.

– Hertfordshire Yeomanry

King Edward VII's favourite residence was Sandringham and particular friend was the Earl of Leicester, the Lord Lieutenant of the county; at the King's express wish a new regiment of Norfolk Yeomanry was raised.

– Suffolk & Norfolk Yeomanry

Photographed at Blenheim Palace, the Berkshire Yeomanry and Queen's Own Oxfordshire Hussars are shown during the Memorial Parade held to commemorate the South African War.

– Berkshire Yeomanry

A Maxim gun section of the Westminster Dragoons in 1908.

– Westminster Dragoons

The experience of the South African war forced the British government and the War Office to adopt a fresh approach towards Imperial defence for the future. Continental warfare in Europe involving non-regular troops was of course barely contemplated, but the formation of the Territorial Force in 1908, central to the reforms introduced by Lord Haldane, resulted in a much more effective organisation of the reserve forces for home defence. At an impressive ceremony in 1909 King Edward VII presented guidons and colours to representative parties from regiments of his newly reorganised Territorial Force, the backbone of which was the Yeomanry and Volunteer regiments.

A patrol of the East Riding Yeomanry during an exercise. Although one of the most junior of the 'new' regiments of Yeomanry, it has always been very strongly imbued with the 'Yeomanry spirit', and its very appropriate badge is retained as the regimental badge of the modern-day Queen's Own Yeomanry.

– The Queen's Own Yorkshire Yeomanry

Relaxing Staffordshire yeomen and a haycart during training before the Great War. The familiar 'four b' two' wrapped around their forage caps indicates that they had recently been 'the enemy' during a 'scheme'.

– Staffordshire Yeomanry/ Major T. H. Gardner

There were 55 regiments of Yeomanry. Their training was now modified in the light of the experience of the Boer War. New equipment was introduced, particularly for specialised sections such as the machine-gun sections, wireless telegraphy sections and for motor transport. Imperial Yeomanry cadet detachments were also formed at this time. Rifle shooting was practised with a new sense of urgency and the regiments now contained a proportion of men who had volunteered for service anywhere in the Empire.

The Worcestershire Yeomanry at annual camp, Emley Castle 1911.

– Worcester City Museum and Art Gallery/ Worcestershire Yeomanry

Berkshire yeomen cleaning tack and equipment at camp in 1913. Sir Osbert Sitwell was to say of a similar camp of the time that . . . 'A certain fascination could be found in leading a life under the greenwood tree. Good humour reigned, partly because this short period constituted to the younger men their annual holiday, to the older an escape from wives and families, partly because to all of them it was a masquerade.' Perhaps all peacetime soldiering is a masquerade of one sort or another.

– Berkshire Yeomanry

5
The First World War

On mobilisation in August 1914 the whole of the Territorial Force concentrated for home defence according to contingency plans. For some time the War Office had an ambivalent attitude towards Territorial regiments serving overseas, despite their contribution to the Boer War. But manpower pressures led first to individual regiments going abroad in 1914, and from 1915 onwards, complete formations.

Those which went to France with the British Expeditionary Force were equipped to fight in the cavalry role and they joined various formations either as complete or as composite regiments. A number of regiments, also in the cavalry role, went to Egypt for the defence of the Suez Canal, but they, and some sent direct from England, were used in dismounted action for the latter part of the Gallipoli campaign. From 1916 the majority of the Yeomanry regiments were in action in Egypt and subsequently Palestine. Extreme shortages of troops in France in the spring of 1918 led to many units moving to the Western Front as infantry or machine-gunners rather than cavalry, in time to take part in the advance in the autumn which resulted in the collapse of Germany.

Representative yeomen, (left) *1914 Trumpeter Wooldridge, 2nd Troop B Squadron of the Middlesex Yeomanry* (middle); *1911 Trooper Dabbs and* (bottom) *a trooper off duty in Egypt, both of the Queen's Own Worcestershire Hussars.*

– Middlesex Yeomanry; Worcester City Museum and Art Gallery/Worcestershire Yeomanry

In the early part of the war all Territorial Force units were instructed to form reserve or 'Second Line' regiments (indicated by 2/ in front of their designation). They remained in the United Kingdom (with onc cxccption), their task being to provide fully trained drafts for the first line regiments abroad and for Home Defence. Most were converted to cyclists in 1916. 'Third Line' regiments were also formed (with 3/ in front of their titles) as training regiments. They were disbanded in February 1917 when cavalry training in the United Kingdom was extensively reorganised.

A trooper of the Essex Yeomanry is seen here in France somewhere in the rear areas. Clearly shown is the 1908 pattern sword, probably the best cavalry sword ever designed.

– Essex Yeomanry

THE WESTERN FRONT

Squadrons of the North Irish and South Irish Horse and the Oxfordshire Hussars were the first to join the BEF in the autumn of 1914. They were joined in due course by other regiments in France. The Cavalry, both Regular and Yeomanry, was kept in reserve for much of the time awaiting opportunities of a breakthrough in the line. Constantly on the move from sector to sector, and waiting in reserve areas near to where major battles were being fought, was a frustrating existence. A steady number of casualties due to the rigours of active service, if not from direct engagement by the enemy, was sustained particularly in the winter months. During a lull in the winter of 1914, the Leicestershire Yeomanry sent for some couples of hounds from the Quorn, Cottesmore and Lord Harrington's Hunts, and several days' sport was enjoyed.

Indeed from time to time every regiment provided reliefs in the trenches, their horses held in reserve well clear of the front line. Casualties inevitably mounted. Constant re-organisation took place as the war progressed and several regiments were re-roled, mainly as infantry, from the summer of 1917 onwards.

Notable engagements were fought, but they were more the exception than the rule. In May 1915, 8 Cavalry Brigade, comprising the Royal Horse Guards, 10th Hussars and the Essex Yeomanry were ordered to carry out a counter-attack on some enemy-held lines. Reaching the start line, the Essex Yeomanry saw a group of some thirty Germans withdrawing rapidly and could scarcely be restrained. 'There was no chance of stopping them or the Tenth, and the whole line went straight on as fast as they could go up hill through the mud, holloaing like mad.' The trenches were captured but, after enduring a counter-bombardment for two hours, the Essex Yeomanry and the Regular regiments were ordered to withdraw.

One proper mounted action was the charge of the Northumberland Hussars at Morlancourt on the Somme in 1918. Crossing a valley at the full gallop to assist the advancing infantry, the leading squadron was checked by a strong German position, with machine-guns defended by wire. It was a gallant charge which served to distract the enemy and enabled the infantry to make local gains, but under these circumstances the effect of such shock action by cavalry could not be expected to be decisive.

This painting shows the charge of the Northumberland Hussars at Morlancourt in August 1918. The opportunities for such a manoeuvre were rare.

– Northumberland Hussars

A number of Yeomanry regiments, moved from the Middle East on the conclusion of the Palestine Campaign, were to fight with distinction and win their share of honours. The VC was awarded in 1918 to Sergeant Caldwell of the Ayrshire Yeomanry for the single-handed capture of an enemy position and the taking of eighteen prisoners. Sergeant Waring of the Montgomeryshire Yeomanry (which formed part of the 25th Bn The Royal Welch Fusiliers) won the same distinction that year for a similar exploit at Reussy.

WAR AGAINST THE TURKS

The defence of the Suez Canal was crucial to Britain's Imperial strategy, and Egypt had been declared a British Protectorate on the outbreak of war with Turkey. A large number of British and Imperial troops was sent there for the defence of the Canal, which included the 2nd Mounted Division which was formed in 1914 and comprised four brigades each of three Yeomanry regiments. Another Yeomanry brigade of two regiments (the Herts Yeomanry and Westminster Dragoons), had arrived in Egypt in the autumn of 1914 to relieve regular garrison troops.

During the last five months of the Gallipoli campaign thirty-one Yeomanry regiments fought as dismounted troops on the peninsula. Kitchener had wanted the whole of the 2nd Mounted Division to move from Egypt to act as immediate reinforcements for Sir Ian Hamilton's invasion of Gallipoli in April 1915. The Commander of the Canal Defences could not spare the Division until August. Leaving rear-parties in Egypt to look after the horses, the 5,000 dismounted yeomen of the Division landed at Suvla Bay on 17–18 August. The 50,000 British and Dominion troops were already hard pressed by a more numerous and rapidly increasing Turkish force.

On 21 August the Battle of Scimitar Hill took place. This hill dominated two others nicknamed Green Hill and Chocolate Hill. The task of the 2nd Mounted Division and the 10th Infantry Division was to pass through the objectives of the first assaulting troops and, after capturing Scimitar Hill, to exploit forward. The advance across the Salt Lake between Suvla and the hills was a noble sight as described by General Hamilton in his despatch: 'During the march, they came under remarkable and accurate artillery fire. The advance of the English yeomen was a sight calculated to send a thrill of pride through anyone with a drop of English blood in their veins. Such superb martial spectacles are rare in modern war. For a mile and a half there was nothing to conceal a mouse, much less some of the most stalwart soldiers England has ever sent from her shores . . . like men marching on parade.'

Brigade and regimental headquarters' staff were in these columns. Brigadier Lord Longford, Brigadier Kenna VC, and Colonel Milbanke VC (commanding the Sherwood Rangers Yeomanry), were killed in action. Trooper Potts of the Berkshire Yeomanry won the VC for remaining with an injured comrade and dragging him back to the line with the aid of a shovel under intense enemy fire. The 2nd Mounted Division received thirty per cent casualties whilst the 2nd Mounted Brigade (Buckinghamshire, Dorset and Berkshire regiments) suffered fifty per cent. But the operation was unsuccessful, and the invasion force had long lost the initiative on this front.

In September and October three Scottish Yeomanry brigades arrived, together with the South-East, South-West and East Mounted Brigades, the latter

Top left
The 3rd (Notts and Derby) Mounted Brigade landed in Gallipoli as part of the 2nd Mounted Division on 17/18th August 1915.

– Sherwood Rangers Yeomanry

Top right
The Headquarters of the Notts and Derby Mounted Brigade showing Captains Delmage (21st Lancers), Milward and Holden (South Notts Hussars), Brigadier General Kenna VC and Captain Lord Hartington (Derbyshire Yeomanry), later the 11th Duke of Devonshire.

– South Notts Hussars

Bottom
Officers of the fourteen Yeomanry regiments being briefed before going into action on the morning of 21st August 1915 at Scimitar Hill, Gallipoli. In a few hours many of these men would be dead or wounded – casualties of a frontal attack, over a large expanse of open ground and formed in columns.

– Hertfordshire Yeomanry

containing the Welsh Horse. They took up positions in the trenches and in November the original Yeomanry regiments left for Egypt. The newly arrived yeomen had to face not only the Turkish enemy but a most fearful gale, which lasted for three days, and blizzards that followed. Thousands of British troops suffered severe frostbite, hundreds were frozen to death or drowned in the flooded trenches. In December and January the British forces finally withdrew.

The campaign in Gallipoli had been fought for some months before Yeomanry brigades were brought in as re-inforcements. The Scottish Horse Brigade, commanded by Lord Tullibardine (later the Duke of Atholl), are seen here digging in by the shore at Suvla Bay in September 1915. The number of men officially required to man each yard of front-line trench was four. The British forces at Anzac and Suvla were holding 20,000 yards with 50,000 rifles. The Turks had 75,000 rifles and 84 guns overlooking the British lines 'like an audience in the dress circle overlooks the stage.'

– The Scottish Horse

The 2nd Mounted Division re-formed as cavalry in Egypt during 1916. The other Yeomanry regiments, which had embarked for Gallipoli direct from England without their horses, also re-formed in Egypt but as infantry battalions, some of them amalgamated. Some regiments, both mounted and dismounted, moved to the Salonika front, but the majority remained in Egypt and most of the Yeomanry infantry regiments were formed into the 74th (Yeomanry) Division, nicknamed the 'Broken Spur' Division. An appreciable number of yeomen from most of the regiments serving in Egypt were accepted for service in the Imperial Camel Corps which took part in many actions in the Middle East campaign.

Operations during 1916 were mainly defensive actions against Turkish and Senussi incursions. Guarding blockhouses, manning trenches and guarding lines of communications were routine matters that had to be undertaken. Those that remained as mounted troops spent much time in patrolling, and some were

A firing trench of the 2nd County of London Yeomanry, (Westminster Dragoons) on the Suez Canal in 1915. The Regiment had arrived in Egypt in late 1914 as a cavalry regiment.

– Westminster Dragoons

engaged in minor actions in the Sinai Desert as the Canal defences were extended eastwards. One of the major problems was to find sufficient supplies of water for men, animals and an increasing number of military vehicles.

The campaign in the Sinai Desert involved 5 Mounted Brigade (formerly 1st South Midlands) comprising the Queen's Own Worcestershire, Royal Gloucestershire Hussars and Warwickshire regiments. They took part in the battle of Romani on the Coast road and the taking of El Arish after its evacuation by the Turks. In January 1917 the same Brigade carried out a mounted attack at Rafa on the Palestine border, although some of the objectives required the yeomen to dismount.

Despite the number of troops on the Bulgarian Front, the Allied effort was chiefly a holding operation. A number of mounted and dismounted Yeomanry Regiments served in Salonika from 1916–1918. These photographs show the horse lines and shoeing-smiths at work.

– South Notts Hussars

A lookout of the Worcester Yeomanry in the Sinai desert in 1916. There had always been a fear that the Turks would mount a determined attack on the Suez Canal and many thousands of troops were detailed for Canal defences for the first two years of the war.

– Worcester City Museum and Art Gallery/ Worcestershire Yeomanry

Other formations now crossed the Sinai Desert ready for the first major attack of the campaign in Palestine – the capture of Gaza, some thirty miles inside the border. Before operations began there was a memorable 'Desert Column Spring Meeting' which included the 'Sinai Grand National' (won by Captain R. F. K. Gooch of the Warwickshire Yeomanry on his remarkable horse Clautoi, which was constantly in action yet survived the war). The races were held on the scene of a recent battle and all the runners had a short time before been in action.

The advance of 5 and 6 Mounted Brigades (Berkshire, Buckinghamshire and Dorset Yeomanry) and the 3rd Australian Light Horse Brigade was successful in cutting the line of communication from the Gaza garrison to the north and east of the town. 22 Mounted Brigade of the Lincoln, Staffordshire and East Riding Yeomanry, fought their way into the outskirts of Gaza, but the town could not be secured and a withdrawal was ordered. The second battle for Gaza was a more

A patrol of the Sussex Yeomanry at Matruh on the Mediterranean coast. The enemy would have been Senussi tribesmen and the yeomen appear to have the use of borrowed horses since they were sent to Egypt (via Gallipoli) as dismounted troops.

– Sussex Yeomanry/Official Photograph

The Queen's Own Dorset Yeomanry at the battle of Agagia, 26th February 1916 against the Senussi tribesmen in Egypt. After a painting by Lady Butler.

– National Army Museum

bloody affair and it too failed. New positions, however, were established near the town, as fresh troops and a new Commander-in-chief, General Sir Edmund Allenby, were awaited.

In the summer of 1917 there was much re-organisation of the Middle East forces. Most of the Yeomanry mounted regiments were concentrated in the 6, 8 and 22 Mounted Brigades of the Yeomanry Mounted Division. This was incorporated into the Desert Mounted Corps. 5 Mounted Brigade was assigned to the Australian Mounted Division, whilst 7 Mounted Brigade were Corps Troops. Yeomanry regiments also provided corps cavalry regiments for the two infantry corps.

In October the third battle of Gaza took place. The Desert Mounted Corps was used to great effect in taking a right-handed sweep into the Beersheba area and outflanking the enemy. At Huj a notable charge was made by the Warwickshire Yeomanry and Worcestershire Yeomanry, a combined total of ten troops, supported by the Royal Gloucestershire Hussars. The Yeomanry reached the

A patrol of the Middlesex Hussars questions an Arab boy: it is recorded that he gave them news of enemy movement. Palestine 1917.

– Middlesex Yeomanry

Queen's Own Worcestershire Hussars watering horses at Cherith, Palestine 1917. Large areas of Palestine were particularly dry and parched and often the horses and men went without water for periods of many hours.

– Worcester City Museum and Art Gallery/ Worcestershire Yeomanry

An artist's impression after the capture of the Turkish guns at Huj illustrates the tasks confronting the victors after an engagement.

– Royal Gloucestershire Hussars

A halt for a patrol of the Duke of Lancaster's Own Yeomanry near Tripoli, Palestine in 1917.

– Duke of Lancaster's Own Yeomanry

Among the first troops into Jerusalem were the Westminster Dragoons.

– Westminster Dragoons

Just before the dismounted attack near Es Salt on 3 May 1918, the Queen's Own Worcestershire Hussars form up in dead ground.

– Worcester City Museum and Art Gallery/ Worcestershire Yeomanry

position and attacked from the flank, charging at the gallop over half a mile of open country. Casualties to both men and horses were heavy, but it was a successful engagement.

A week later, on 13 November, 6 Mounted Brigade performed a remarkable attack at El Mughar, west of Jerusalem and close to the sea. The brigade was ordered to take a Turkish position which was at the top of a long slope. It formed up with the Buckinghamshire Yeomanry and Dorset Yeomanry in the lead and the Berkshire Yeomanry in reserve, covered by Royal Horse Artillery. Whereas on the left the Buckinghamshire Yeomanry could approach the position and carry out the attack with the sword at speed, the leading squadron of the Dorset Yeomanry dismounted and charged on foot with rifle and bayonet. The Berkshire Yeomanry cleared the enemy's depth position, but while fighting through the village, they too had to dismount. Successes such as these proved the effective use of shock action by cavalry against infantry, such as had rarely been possible on the Western Front.

Allenby's mounted divisions exploited the breakthrough and a rapid advance was made on Jerusalem which fell to the Allies before Christmas 1917.

In the Spring of 1918, the 74th (Yeomanry) Division and some of the other Yeomanry regiments were moved to France. The remaining mounted regiments took part in the closing stages of the Palestine campaign, including the battles of Sharon and Meggido and the advance to and capture of Damascus.

6
1919–1945

After the war it was clear that a radically different reserve army was required, and a commission was set up to decide upon the re-organisation of the Territorial Force. Honorary colonels and commanding officers of the Yeomanry regiments were given some consideration when the future of the regiments was being determined. The decision was that the fourteen senior regiments in the official table of precedence were to remain as cavalry, and the Lovat Scouts and Scottish

A detachment of Royal Devon Yeomanry at camp in the 1920s.

– Royal Devon Yeomanry

389 (Sussex Yeomanry). Battery of 78th (Surrey & Sussex Yeomanry) Brigade, R.F.A. on the move at Fontwell Park in 1926. Until fully converted to tractor or lorry-towed guns, the Yeomanry Gunner batteries still kept substantial numbers of horses on their establishment.

– Sussex Yeomanry/Official Photograph

The East Riding Yeomanry was reduced to one squadron and converted to an armoured car company of the Royal Tank Corps. The squadron is seen here at camp.

– The Queen's Own Yorkshire Yeomanry

The Leicestershire Yeomanry demonstration ride of 1923.

– Leicestershire and Derbyshire Yeomanry

For those regiments who were retained as cavalry, training continued much the same as before the Great War. These photographs show the Royal Wiltshire Yeomanry at camp in 1934 with (left) *C Squadron on the march and* (right) *A Squadron watering horses.*

– Royal Wiltshire Yeomanry

Horse were retained mounted as 'scouts'. Some measure of choice was allowed to the remainder. Twenty-five regiments chose conversion to artillery, chiefly for the reason that it enabled them to retain horses, since there were no plans as yet to mechanise the artillery. Most were incorporated into brigades of the Royal Field Artillery (RFA), later becoming Field Regiments Royal Artillery (RA).

Eight regiments were reduced in strength and became armoured car companies of the Tank Corps ('Royal' from 1923). One regiment was absorbed into its local

Top & bottom left
Scarcely nowhere else in the British Army was the dictum so strongly held than in the Yeomanry – that military matters should never seriously be allowed to intervene between a sportsman and his sport. An officer of the Scottish Horse takes time off during Camp to fish on the Blair Atholl estate during the '30s and a group of Sherwood Rangers are photographed with their bag of duck in Palestine in 1940.

– Scottish Horse/Sherwood Rangers Yeomanry

Bottom right
Major-General Blakiston-Houston (second from right), *the Inspector General of Cavalry, visits the Derbyshire Yeomanry Armoured Car Company in the field in 1934.*

– Sherwood Rangers Yeomanry

infantry battalion, one became a signals regiment attached to a cavalry division and two were disbanded.

The composition of the 'Territorial Army' (TA), as the Territorial Force was renamed, was changing with society. Even those regiments which had transferred to other arms maintained their special Yeomanry prestige and spirit to a greater or lesser extent. They continued to train hard, learn the new equipment and adapt to the current tactical concepts, which were not entirely retrospective.

With the prospect growing of another war it was clear by the autumn of 1938 that an expansion of the Territorial Army was essential. Already the formation of more anti-aircraft units had begun and this included Yeomanry artillery regiments. Early in 1939 it was announced that the whole of the Territorial Army Field Force – the infantry divisions with their supporting divisions – was to be doubled, and so-called 'duplicate' units were formed, intended for front-line service.

Royal Devon Yeomanry at Firing Camp at Larkhill in 1938. This practice was clearly fired at tank targets over open sights, a technique which was to prove necessary for field as well as anti-tank gunners in the 2nd World War.

– Royal Devon Yeomanry

These privately adapted Morris Cowley 'armoured machine gun carriers' were owned by the Inns of Court Regiment in 1932/3. They 'restored mobility . . . thus making practicable exercises between the two infantry companies and the mounted squadron.'

– Inns of Court and City Yeomanry

THE BRITISH EXPEDITIONARY FORCE

A number of Yeomanry regiments went to France in 1939 with the British Expeditionary Force. Three fought in tanks, including the Yorkshire Dragoons, the 1st Lothians and Border Horse, whose task was part of a covering force some miles east of the Maginot Line, and the 1st Fife and Forfar Yeomanry. The two Denbighshire Yeomanry medium artillery regiments, the 78th (Surrey and Sussex Yeomanry) and 97th (Kent Yeomanry) Field Regiments and the 79th (Herts Yeomanry) Heavy Anti-Aircraft Regiment were also deployed in France. During the German offensive in May 1940 the Surrey Yeomanry was concentrated in the Hazebrouck and Bailleul area whilst the Herts Yeomanry provided air defence for Le Havre. The 64 (Queen's Own Royal Glasgow Yeomanry) Anti-Tank Regiment served in the Cherbourg area before withdrawal.

The confusion and hardship of the retreating army is well illustrated by accounts of the Kent Yeomanry. Having been ordered to withdraw a number of times and then cover a counter-attack which never took place, the Regiment was instructed to hold the line near Warneton close to the Belgian–French border. This meant that the line had to be held by the guns alone without infantry cover. The 3rd Battalion, the Grenadier Guards appeared unexpectedly and put in a counter-attack which stabilised the line successfully for one more day, before the order to withdraw was given.

A proportion of all regiments came out of France, but many of the Yeomanry regiments, like most units that came through Dunkirk, were severely depleted. In due course they were re-formed, re-equipped, and trained either for the defence of Britain or for further service overseas.

The Warwickshire Yeomanry is seen in this photograph on patrol at Rosh Pinna, Syria in 1940.

– Imperial War Museum

Watering horses, a Stafford yeoman with mounts in Syria.

– **Staffordshire Yeomanry/ Major T. H. Gardner**

THE MIDDLE EAST

A number of the Yeomanry regiments were sent to the Middle East in the early months of the War, eight of them in the cavalry role. With two regular regiments they made up the 1st Cavalry Division, which later was redesignated 10th Armoured Division.

The only cavalry action before mechanisation was complete took place in the Syrian Campaign, where the Vichy French forces were posing a threat to British control of the Eastern Mediterranean countries. 5 Cavalry Brigade, comprising, inter alia, the North Somerset Yeomanry, the Yorkshire Dragoons and the Cheshire (Earl of Chester's) Yeomanry spent much time patrolling against a withdrawing enemy. The last mounted actions fought by British cavalry were in the River Litani area. On 9 June 1941 the Cheshire Yeomanry formed up with others to capture a strongly held bridge. The enemy withdrew and the bridge was taken. Two days later the regiment again forced the enemy to withdraw from a strong position – the threat of cavalry in its traditional role as the arm of shock action was enough to unnerve the enemy. The last mounted regiment in action were the Yorkshire Dragoons, on 10 July 1941.

A succession of exploits, which well illustrates the versatility and stamina of the Yeomanry, was that of the Kingcol force of the Royal Wiltshire Yeomanry, the Warwickshire Yeomanry and Household Cavalry Regiment. Having given up their horses they set off in lorries, with whatever arms could be supplied, across the scorching Syrian desert to destroy the Iraqi rebels who threatened Baghdad. This accomplished, they returned to Syria and became heavily involved in the campaign, where they were continually bombed by the Vichy French. They returned to Iraq and were then sent to Teheran, entering the city at the same time as the Russian allies.

104th (Essex Yeomanry) Field Regiment RA fought at Tobruk. Here a 25 pr gun is seen in action in the desert in 1941.

– Essex Yeomanry

THE WESTERN DESERT

It was realised in 1940 that the Axis powers were planning a pincer attack on British-held Egypt from Ethiopia and Italian Somaliland in the south and Libya in the west. To meet this threat, particularly from Libya, an immediate build-up of troops was required, and the rapid deployment of regiments equipped with tanks was vital. A number of Yeomanry regiments was moved to Egypt, issued with tanks, and deployed westwards into Libya. Tank formations and tactics had to be learnt, wireless procedures mastered, never-ending maintenance of the tanks and wheeled vehicles carried out, and re-supply problems overcome. Co-operation with other arms had to be practised again and again, and all in extreme conditions of climate and terrain. Regiments often had as many as three different types of tanks, an enormous problem for logistical support.

From secure bases in Tripoli, with short lines of communication across the Mediterranean and with tanks superior in armour, fire-power and mechanical reliability, the Axis commander, Rommel, campaigned successfully in 1941–2. Nevertheless the Eighth Army, composed of British and Commonwealth divisions, inflicted their first defeat of German troops in the war during the 'Crusader' offensive in November 1941. 22 Armoured Brigade, comprising the Royal Gloucestershire Hussars and the 3rd and 4th County of London Yeomanry, fought fierce actions in the areas around the two airfields at El Gubi and Sidi-Rezegh in an attempt to relieve Tobruk.

But with the German tanks outgunning the British and with the necessity of withdrawing to a line that could be held in strength, it was clearly going to be a huge task to go on the offensive, let alone push back and destroy the German Afrika Corps and the Italian forces.

The turning point came with the battle of Alam El Halfa from 31 August to 7 September 1942. 22 Armoured Brigade were again employed and were joined by 8 Armoured Brigade comprising the Staffordshire Yeomanry, the Sherwood Rangers Yeomanry and the 3rd Royal Tank Regiment. Their task was to support positions overlooking the minefield, and, in particular to guard against a flank

There was intensive training during the Summer of 1942 prior to the battle of El Alamein. Staffordshire yeomen are shown filling machine gun belts.

– Official Photographs/ Major T. H. Gardner

A Crusader tank of the Sherwood Rangers in October 1942. The temporary tank commander is Major General A. H. Gatehouse who commanded the 10th Armoured Division at Alamein in which the Regiment served.

– Sherwood Rangers Yeomanry

attack by armoured troops. The battle lasted for many hours and the advance of Rommel's Afrika Corps was finally stemmed. The success of the battle enabled the Eighth Army first to consolidate and then prepare to go over to the offensive.

The Battle of El Alamein, which started at 9.40 on 23 October 1942, involved a number of Yeomanry regiments. The Yorkshire Dragoons fought as lorried infantry with 1st Armoured Division; 8 Armoured Brigade was comprised as before. 7th Armoured Division included the 4th County of London Yeomanry (Sharpshooters) in tanks and the 2nd Derbyshire Yeomanry in armoured cars. The Royal Wiltshire Yeomanry and Warwickshire Yeomanry were in 9 Armoured Brigade and the depleted 2nd Royal Gloucestershire Hussars were used to reinforce other regiments. In addition to these regiments there were six

The crew of a Grant tank called 'Robin Hood' brew up in the desert. Lieutenant General Sir Brian Horrocks, who had the Sherwood Rangers under his command from August 1942 to May 1945, was to say of the Regiment 'I shall maintain that the Sherwood Rangers Yeomanry took part in more fighting than did any other armoured regiment during this period'.

– Imperial War Museum

El Alamein – Staffordshire Yeomanry Crusader tanks moving across the desert at speed towards the enemy positions.

– Official photograph/Major T. H. Gardner

A Crusader tank of the Royal Wiltshire Yeomanry advances through loose sand in North Africa. The Regiment had three different types of tanks at the same time during the campaign. Resupply and repair problems can be imagined.

– Royal Wiltshire Yeomanry

Churchill tanks of the North Irish Horse are depicted here by a broken railway line at Ksar Mesoura, Egypt.

– Imperial War Museum

Yeomanry artillery regiments, the Surrey and Sussex, Kent, Norfolk, Lancashire Hussars, Essex and Denbighshire.

9 Armoured Brigade, which was part of the 1st New Zealand Division, were spearhead troops whose task it was to advance through the minefields between the opposing armies. The fiercest resistance was put up by the Germans and Italians and the battle raged through the next ten days, the tanks constantly in action and the artillery relentlessly bombarding the Axis formations. The success of the Battle of El Alamein was due in part to the long lines of Rommel's communications, but meticulous preparation, timing and the confidence of an Army on the offensive gave the Allies the moral advantage in battle.

THE ITALIAN CAMPAIGN

With the successful advance through Libya and the destruction of the German and Italian forces in Tunisia, the Eighth Army formed part of the assault on Sicily and subsequent landings in and the advance through Italy. Armour was used extensively and included a number of Yeomanry regiments such as the 3rd County of London Yeomanry (Sharpshooters) and the Warwickshire Yeomanry.

A detachment of 148th (Bedfordshire Yeomanry) Field Regiment RA 'take post' during a live firing exercise in Wales July 1941. The Regiment soon after was sent to Singapore and was captured by the Japanese.

– Imperial War Museum/ Bedfordshire Yeomanry

For those regiments who did not serve overseas until later in the war, training was nevertheless intense. The Lovat Scouts, seen here on training in Canada, were given a mountain patrol role and they subsequently were sent to Italy.

– Lovat Scouts

The close terrain was in contrast to that of the Western Desert; much of the fighting was at troop level and at almost point-blank range. Yeomanry artillery regiments in this theatre included the Royal Devon Yeomanry and the 102nd (Northumberland Hussars) Anti-Tank Regiment.

The advance through Italy required close co-operation between armour and infantry. The many famous engagements in which the Yeomanry regiments were involved included Taranto, Salerno, Anzio, Termoli, Cassino, the Moro river, Lake Trasimene, the advance on Rome and the breakthrough of the Gothic and Gustav Lines.

At the Battle of Termoli, the action of a single gun of the Glasgow Yeomanry, the 64th Anti-Tank Regiment, showed the courage and devotion to duty of the yeoman gunners. All but one of the crew were casualties and the armoured reconnaissance squadron, which the yeomen were supporting, was ordered to withdraw. The remaining gunner refused to leave his gun and, helped by a trooper from the squadron, covered the withdrawal by firing round after round at the approaching enemy armour. Both men were killed, but the enemy withdrew.

The Battle for Monte Cassino lasted from January to May 1944 and proved to be the Germans' most determined resistance of the campaign. Although the infantry was to bear the brunt of the fighting to capture the ground which dominated the route to Rome, many artillery regiments, including some yeomen gunners, fought in the battle. The Surrey and Sussex Yeomanry served in Priest SP-guns and manned an OP during the battle on Mount Trochio from which the whole of the area could be seen. The Ayrshire Yeomanry had their gun positions lower down on the same mountain. Many casualties were sustained on the road approaching the gun positions which were exposed to enemy artillery fire. The gunners' task was to provide a constant bombardment of smoke and HE to try to minimise the effectiveness of the enemy artillery fire.

The stiffest battle in the campaign for the Kent Yeomanry was undoubtedly on the Senio river, to the North of Rome and near the Adriatic Coast. In appalling weather during December 1944 the Regiment was in support of the attacking 10th Indian and New Zealand Divisions. The Kent yeoman had to provide fire support for the infantry for nearly two days before all the objectives were taken.

THE FAR EAST

None of the mounted or armoured Yeomanry regiments fought in the Far East but early in the campaign in Malaya, three artillery regiments – the 155th (Lanarkshire Yeomanry) Field Regiment, the 148th (Bedfordshire Yeomanry) Field Regiment and 135th (Hertfordshire Yeomanry) Field Regiments – were sent to fight against the Japanese. These regiments were all lost as the enemy

An SP gun of 147 (Essex Yeomanry) Field Regiment RA on Le Hamel beach at about H + 60 minutes on D Day.

– Imperial War Museum/ Essex Yeomanry

Sherman Tanks of the 2nd Fife and Forfar Yeomanry at Bayeux, Normandy in June 1944. Soon afterwards the Regiment suffered severe casualties during Operation Goodwood.

– Imperial War Museum

advanced through Malaya and captured Singapore.

414 (Essex Yeomanry) Battery, RHA, fought for some months in Burma in 1942 during the withdrawal. The 145 (Berkshire Yeomanry) Field Regiment and the 96th (Royal Devon Yeomanry) Field Regiment were both sent to India in 1945. They did not arrive, however, in time to be sent into action before VJ Day.

The 99th (Bucks Yeomanry) Field Regiment had been in action in the Arakan expedition in Burma in 1942 and took part in the desperate battle of Kohima with the 2nd Division which halted the Japanese advance into India.

NORTH-WEST EUROPE

The order of battle of the British invasion force in June 1944 included many Yeomanry armoured and artillery regiments. Amongst the first troops ashore on D-Day were the Sherwood Rangers Yeomanry who landed in Sherman DD amphibious tanks, and the Staffordshire Yeomanry who, on the first day, accounted for seven enemy tanks destroyed and two disabled for the loss of five Shermans. One 88mm German gun – a weapon that proved deadly to allied armour time and again throughout the war – accounted for the Staffordshire's losses.

These two photographs show Sherman tanks of the Staffordshire Yeomanry in the Caen sector in late June 1944: (Above) *tanks at the start line before an attack and* (below) *moving forward across country.*

– Official Photographs/ Major T. H. Gardner

A Sherman tank of the East Riding Yeomanry passing through Rouen en route to St Valery, August 1944.

– The Queen's Own Yorkshire Yeomanry

The Yeomanry regiments which landed on D-Day were the East Riding Yeomanry, two batteries of the Northumberland Hussars, the Herts Yeomanry and Essex Yeomanry both with self-propelled guns, and C Squadron of the Inns of Court Regiment. 12th Battalion The Parachute Regiment, which included some former East Riding yeomen, dropped with the 6th Airborne Division.

The Essex Yeomanry began firing their SP guns while they were still embarked on the landing craft from H minus 35 and within those thirty-five minutes had fired about 3,500 rounds. The landing was far from easy and many of the vehicles were lost; but the regiment was able to resume firing at H plus 60.

The 2nd Derbyshire Yeomanry, a divisional reconnaissance regiment, who had gained their reconnaissance experience in the Desert, landed on D plus 1 but initially were used in guard duties on the 'Pegasus' Bridge on the River Orne. Subsequently they took part in the assault on Caen, and also supported the 51st Highland Division in an attack on the Colombelles industrial area near Caen, held by the Germans in great strength. Later the regiment was called upon to perform tasks for many different British and Allied formations and units as the advance progressed across Northern France.

During June a number of other Yeomanry armoured and artillery regiments landed on the Normandy Beaches and took part in the Campaign across Northern France. The toughest fighting in July 1944 was during Operation Goodwood – the attempted break-out from the Caen bridgehead – when the Germans hastily massed as much armour as was available in a desperate attempt to contain the Allies. The 2nd Fife and Forfar Yeomanry fought without a break during the whole of the battle, losing most of its tanks and 100 men.

A Sexton 25 pr self-propelled gun of 86 (Herts Yeomanry) Field Regiment RA advances after the breakout towards the Seine in August 1944.

– Herts Yeomanry

Sherman tanks of the 1st Lothian and Border Horse halted at Geilenkirchen.

– Imperial War Museum

Right
A Sherman of 3/4 County of London Yeomanry (Sharpshooters) at Brunen March 1945.

– Official Photograph/Major T. H. Gardner

Left
DD Shermans of the Staffordshire Yeomanry after the crossing of the Elbe in Germany in 1945. It was vital for armoured support for the infantry to be close at hand during assault river crossings at each stage in the campaign in North-West Europe, and many regiments were equipped with 'duplex-drive' tanks for just this purpose.

– National Army Museum

An officer of the South Nottinghamshire Yeomanry Cavalry 1803 by an unknown artist.
— Sherwood Rangers Yeomanry.

An Officer and Trumpeter of the Northumberland Hussars. Painted by J. Mathews in 1893.
— Northumberland Hussars.

Officers of the Yorkshire Hussars, drawn by H. Martens, engraved by J. Harris, published by Fores as one of a series of 1846.
—The Queen's Own Yorkshire Yeomanry.

The Lancashire Hussars, c. 1880. An engraving after Orlando Norrie.
—Wellington College/Colonel H.C.B. Rogers.

The Royal Wiltshire Yeomanry Centenary Inspection by HRH The Prince of Wales in 1894
—The Royal Wiltshire Yeomanry.

A Yeomanry Scout in South Africa. Painted by Lady Butler.
—The Staff College, Camberley.

Colonel A.J. Palmer DSO TD commanding the Royal Gloucestershire Hussars 1899–1923. Painted by J. Mathews in 1902.
— Royal Gloucestershire Hussars.

An officer, 3rd County of London Yeomanry (Sharpshooters). Painted by R. Simkin.
—Kent and Sharpshooters Yeomanry.

The charge of the 6th Mounted Brigade at El Mughar—13 November 1917. The Royal Bucks Hussars are seen here attacking the Turks; to their left were the Dorsets and the Berks Yeomanry were in support. The Berks RHA provided artillery support. Painted by J.P. Beadle.
— The Staff College, Camberley.

Lieutenant Colonel of the City of London Yeomanry (Rough Riders) 1911.
—Inns of Court and City Yeomanry.

The Scottish Horse hunting in Salonika on the Bulgarian Front in 1917. Painted by Lionel Edwards.

—The Scottish Horse.

The 2nd Fife and Forfar Yeomanry are seen here giving covering fire to infantry on the river Elbe, Germany in early 1945. The Regiment had been re-equipped with Comet tanks.

– Imperial War Museum

A 'Crab' flail tank of the Lothians and Border Horse at the landings on the River Walcheren.

– The Tank Museum

Its sister regiment, the 1st Fife and Forfar Yeomanry, had been training on Crocodile flame-thrower tanks for many months, and supporting the 51st Highland Division in Holland, they used them to great effect in numerous actions. The effect of flame-throwing tanks was devasting to enemy infantry at ranges up to 100 yards, although the risks were considerable to the tank crews themselves.

The Allied advance into Germany reached the major obstacle of the River Rhine in early 1945. The Staffordshire Yeomanry, having been specially trained in DD tanks, was in support of the 51st Highland Division whose task was to consolidate a bridgehead on the east bank near the town of Rees. As a result of detailed planning and accurate reconnaissance, this formidable task was accomplished during the night of 23/24 March.

After the German surrender in April, a number of Yeomanry regiments were to remain as troops of Occupation for many months. During the whole war, however, no less than 77 regiments of yeomen had served and almost all of them had fought overseas, thousands of men being killed or wounded in action. Their contribution to the defeat of Britain's enemies in all major theatres had been conspicuous, and there is no doubt that the spirit of belonging to the Yeomanry played a great part in sustaining their morale while in action.

7
1945 to the Present

Comet tanks of the Westminster Dragoons on exercise in 1952.

– The Westminster Dragoons

In 1947 the Territorial Army was reconstituted, but the subsequent history of the Yeomanry regiments continued to be one of constant change. There were 26 regiments of the re-formed Royal Armoured Corps, TA, and 24 regiments of Royal Artillery, TA (there had been altogether 53 regiments of yeomen gunners during the war). The RAC regiments differed in composition and role. There were 'armoured regiments' equipped mainly with Comet tanks and later Centurion tanks, 'divisional regiments', which had the role of reconnaissance and later anti-tank defence in addition, equipped chiefly with Cromwell tanks and half-track personnel carriers, later with Archer (Valentine tanks with 17-pounder anti-tank guns) and Charioteer (Cromwell tanks with 20-pounder guns); and armoured car regiments equipped with Daimler armoured cars and Dingo scout cars. The Yeomanry Gunner regiments comprised all the different types of artillery.

Major reorganisations of the TA took place in 1951, 1956 and 1961. Many of the RAC regiments were amalgamated and most gunner regiments also were amalgamated, redesignated and given new roles. During the years of National

Service a number of regiments provided the continuation training for National Servicemen and reservists.

The greatest reorganisation of all took place in 1967. The majority of Territorial Army regiments were then reduced or disbanded and those which remained were divided into four categories of the Territorial Army and Volunteer Reserve, (TA&VR), with different terms of service and commitment. Some Yeomanry regiments struggled on as TA&VR III regiments but, starved of equipment and funding, they inevitably dwindled. Others managed to retain cadres – establishments of a few officers and NCOs – but most of the remaining

As a divisional Regiment RAC the Royal Wiltshire Yeomanry were equipped with a variety of armoured vehicles after the war. Here an 'Archer' SP anti-tank gun is seen at practice on the range at Kirkcudbright in 1953.

– Royal Wiltshire Yeomanry

A recovery task for yeomen of the Northumberland Hussars on exercise in the '50s.

– Northumberland Hussars

Dingo Scout Cars of the Royal Gloucestershire Hussars preparing for an exercise, photographed outside their Drill Hall at Stroud in 1958.

– The Royal Gloucestershire Hussars

Yeomanry establishments were of sub-unit size. A new major unit of the RAC was formed, named the Royal Yeomanry Regiment, and it comprised the Royal Wiltshire, Sherwood Rangers, Kent and Sharpshooters, North Irish Horse and Berkshire and Westminster Dragoons Squadrons. It was given an armoured reconnaissance role. In 1971 a second armoured reconnaissance regiment was formed – The Queen's Own Yeomanry – comprising the Yorkshire, Ayrshire, Cheshire and Northumberland Hussars Squadrons. In the same year three RAC home defence infantry Yeomanry regiments were formed. The Wessex Yeomanry (later 'Royal') was established with re-formed squadrons of Royal Wiltshire, Royal Gloucestershire Hussars and Royal Devon Yeomanry. The Queen's Own Mercian Yeomanry was formed by incorporating Warwickshire and Worcestershire, Staffordshire and Shropshire Yeomanry squadrons. The third such regiment was a re-formed Duke of Lancaster's Own Yeomanry. In 1983, their role changed again to light recce for home defence.

The Yeomanry who now remain as artillery and signals form one full regiment for each arm, with a number of sub-units which are part of other regiments of the Territorial Army. The artillery regiment is 100th (Yeomanry) Field Regiment RA(V), and comprises batteries of South Notts Hussars, Hertfordshire and Bedfordshire, and Suffolk and Norfolk Yeomanry. 71st (Yeomanry) Signal Regiment (V) is formed with four squadrons, Berkshire, Inns of Court and City Yeomanry and two squadrons of Kent and Sharpshooters Yeomanry.

Ten years ago, when this book was first written, NATO faced the Warsaw Pact at a time when the Cold War seemed set to continue into the far distant future. Plans for nuclear and *blitzkrieg* warfare were drawn up for decades into the new century. Now with the extraordinary recent events in eastern Europe, the Middle East, the Gulf region, the Mediterranean littoral and elsewhere, the armed forces of Britain have faced rapid and radical changes in role and composition. For instance the regular infantry is being cut by twenty-five percent and the Royal Armoured Corps by a massive forty percent. While this is no vehicle to discuss the wisdom or otherwise of the 'Options for Change' exercise, it is at least satisfying

A Fox armoured reconnaissance vehicle of the Yorkshire Squadron, The Queen's Own Yeomanry.

– Official photograph

The assault troop of the Yorkshire Yeomanry Squadron, mounted in Saracen armoured personnel carriers and Ferret Scout cars, move out of barracks in 1975.

– Official Photograph

to note that the Territorial Army has fared reasonably well in terms of reduction.

The Yeomanry has had to face re-organisation too, but based on its traditions of mobility, good communications and local knowledge, the role of National Defence has been enhanced and resulted in expansion in some districts. While some units adopted new roles in 1992–93, and the Queen's Own Mercian Yeomanry and Duke of Lancaster's Own Yeomanry have amalgamated to form the Royal Mercian and Lancastrian Yeomanry, a new regiment – the Scottish Yeomanry – has been formed in the northern kingdom amid great satisfaction.

The Queen's Own Yeomanry is equipped with Scimitar armoured tracked vehicles, and its role is in support of the new Allied Command Europe Rapid Reaction Corps, available for deployment anywhere from Norway to Turkey. Some Royal Artillery and Royal Signals Yeomanry regiments also have a role in the Rapid Reaction Corps. Royal Engineer and Royal Logistic Corps Yeomanry units continue to serve, and the four Land Rover-borne Royal Armoured Corps Yeomanry regiments are assigned to each military district in the UK for National Defence reconnaissance.

While facing the radically new and uncertain conditions in what has been called a post-military age, the Yeomanry in its bi-centenary year continues to be a very distinct arm of Britain's Territorial Army – itself a very valuable part of the most sophisticated, efficient and globally respected armed services for their size of all the nations of the world.

Part II
THE COUNTY REGIMENTS

The County Regiments

Various orders of dress are worn by these officers of twenty-nine Yeomanry regiments. It is believed that this photograph is of the detachment commanders at the Coronation of George V.

– Berkshire Yeomanry

The regiments of Yeomanry are listed in Part II of this book by county. The word 'Corps' was used in the early days to denote either an independent troop or a number of troops under a single command. Squadrons in most regiments did not emerge until the latter part of the nineteenth century.

Precedence of the Yeomanry Cavalry regiments, as can be imagined, has always been a controversial matter. Several lists were drawn up in 1884 and 1885 by the War Office.

The rules for establishing precedence, and they were not adhered to in every case, were according to the date of commissioning of the first troop of the regiment and unbroken service, including both official service and *accepted* unpaid service. Disbanded regiments automatically lost precedence.

The subject of precedence can be followed in the various Army Lists and in Benson Freeman's *History of the South Notts Hussars* Appendix D. The official Order of Precedence of the Yeomanry of the Territorial Force, as shown in the Army List of 1914, is:

1. Royal Wiltshire
2. Warwickshire
3. Yorkshire Hussars
4. Nottinghamshire (Sherwood Rangers)
5. Staffordshire
6. Shropshire
7. Ayrshire
8. Cheshire
9. Yorkshire Dragoons
10. Leicestershire
11. North Somerset
12. Duke of Lancaster's Own
13. Lanarkshire
14. Northumberland
15. Nottinghamshire Hussars, South
16. Denbighshire
17. Westmorland and Cumberland
18. Pembroke
19. Royal East Kent
20. Hampshire
21. Buckinghamshire
22. Derbyshire
23. Dorset
24. Gloucestershire
25. Herts
26. Berks
27. 1st County of London (Middlesex Hussars)
28. Royal 1st Devon
29. Suffolk
30. Royal North Devon
31. Worcestershire
32. West Kent
33. West Somerset
34. Oxfordshire
35. Montgomeryshire
36. Lothians and Border Horse
37. Lanarkshire (Glasgow)
38. Lancashire Hussars
39. Surrey
40. Fife and Forfar
41. Norfolk
42. Sussex
43. Glamorgan
44. Welsh Horse
45. Lincolnshire
46. City of London (Rough Riders)
47. 2nd County of London (Westminster Dragoons)
48. 3rd County of London (Sharpshooters)
49. Bedfordshire
50. Essex
51. Northamptonshire
52. East Riding of Yorkshire
53. 1st Lovat's Scouts
54. 2nd Lovat's Scouts
55. Scottish Horse

The Special Reserve Regiments took precedence after the Reserve Regiments of Cavalry and before the Yeomanry.

This section is mainly concerned with the history of individual regiments carried through the Great War by the First Line regiments. The outline history of the Second-line and Third-line regiments can be found in *British Regiments, 1914–1918* by Brigadier E. A. James.

Terminology has been employed as accurately as possible. The distinction between 'amalgamated' and 'absorbed' is sometimes obscure. The latter term has been used when a Yeomanry regiment has joined an existing unit, and a redesignation in most cases has followed.

The difficulties in settling for a name for each Yeomanry regiment or corps will be understood by sympathetic readers. Just as the number of regiments fluctuated, and dates taken from different sources often conflict, so the Yeomanry regiments constantly changed their names to reflect their composition, role, location, patronage, or, indeed, whim. The names used are mainly those existing at the start of the Great War, and are likely to be the most familiar. The comprehensive derivations of the names can be found in the work by J. B. M. Frederick *Lineage Book of the British Army*.

ANGLESEY

See under Caernarvonshire.

ANGUS (FORFAR)

Yeomanry Calvary were commissioned in December 1794, but little is known thereafter. There are records of attempts to form troops of Yeomanry Cavalry in the County by Lord Airlie in 1831, but it is not certain whether they were raised.

The Forfarshire Yeomanry was re-formed in 1846 but disbanded in 1862. Later in the century the Forfar Light Horse was formed. (See under Fifeshire.)

AYRSHIRE

The Ayrshire Yeomanry (Earl of Carrick's Own)

The Carrick Troop was accepted in 1798 (but probably existed earlier), and was increased to three troops in 1803. The name 'Ayrshire Yeomanry Cavalry' appears in this year and the number of troops was further increased. In 1817 two regiments were formed, the 1st Regiment commanded by Colonel Sir Alexander Boswell, son of Dr Samuel Johnson's biographer. They were constantly involved in giving aid to the Civil Power during this period. The Ayrshire Yeomanry were represented with the Lanarkshire Yeomanry in the 17th Company of the 6th Bn, Imperial Yeomanry, for service in South Africa.

The Regiment landed in Gallipoli in October 1915 and, on the withdrawal, moved to Egypt for dismounted service. In 1917 the 12th (Ayr and Lanark Yeomanry) Bn, the Royal Scots Fusiliers was formed and fought in Palestine. In May 1918 the Battalion was sent to France and fought on the Western Front for the last six months of the war.

The Ayrshire Yeomanry was re-formed as a cavalry regiment and retained the role until 1940 when it formed the 151st and 152nd (Ayrshire Yeomanry) Field Regiments, RA. The former Regiment remained in the United Kingdom until 1944 and landed on the Normandy beaches on 13 June 1944, subsequently fighting in north-west Europe until the end of the War. Elements of 152 Field Regiment served in Orkney and Shetland for a time before the whole Regiment was moved to North Africa in 1942, where it was constantly in action. In February 1944 it landed in Italy and fought throughout the campaign including the action at Monte Cassino.

The Regiment was re-formed as an armoured regiment in 1947 and subsequently was given the armoured delivery role. In 1961 two squadrons were converted to reconnaissance and, after the reductions of the TA in 1967, the Ayrshire Yeomanry provided one squadron for the newly formed Queen's Own Yeomanry in 1971, and now serve in the Scottish Yeomanry.

BEDFORDSHIRE

The Bedfordshire Yeomanry

Authority was given for a troop to be formed in Bedfordshire in 1794, but it was not until 1797 that one was raised. By 1798 four troops were in being: they served through the Peace of Amiens and were consolidated to form a regiment in 1803.

Lord Alwyne Compton, brother of the Marquess of Northampton, served in the 10th Hussars and raised the 28th (Bedfordshire) Company IY. He is seen here in the Lancer Uniform of the Bedfordshire Imperial Yeomanry.

– Bedfordshire Yeomanry

Disbandment of individual troops, however, took place at intervals and by 1810 the Bedfordshire Yeomanry Cavalry had ceased to exist.

In 1817 two new troops were raised and by 1820 six were established. The Regiment was disbanded in 1827. Two troops of the Huntingdonshire Mounted Rifles (The Duke of Manchester's Light Horse) were raised in Bedford and Sharnbrook in 1860. The 28th (Bedfordshire) Company, Imperial Yeomanry, sometimes known as 'Compton's Horse', was raised for service in South Africa in 1900; and this Company provided a nucleus for a new regiment raised in 1901 as the Bedfordshire Imperial Yeomanry.

After serving in Home Forces until June 1915, the Regiment joined 9 Cavalry Brigade in France, with which it served until the end of the war. It retained its horses although most of the time was spent on dismounted duty. For the last few months of the war the Regiment was dispersed to the three Regular regiments of the Brigade, and were much in use during the final advance in the autumn of 1918 in the mounted role.

In 1920 the Bedfordshire Yeomanry was converted to artillery and re-formed as 105 (Bedfordshire Yeomanry) Brigade RFA, later 105th Field Regiment. In 1939 the Regiment was 'duplicated' to form in addition 148th (Bedfordshire

Yeomanry) Field Regiment RA, the original unit becoming 52nd (Bedfordshire Yeomanry) Heavy Regiment, RA, on mobilisation. In the heavy role, it fought with the BEF and was disbanded shortly after evacuation from Dunkirk in 1940. Re-raised in 1943, the Regiment took part in the campaign in north-west Europe. 419 Battery gained particular distinction by giving long-range support to the airborne troops at Arnhem.

148th Field Regiment took part in the defence of Singapore Island with 18th Infantry Division and was captured following the surrender.

On the re-formation of the TA in 1947, the Bedfordshire Yeomanry provided 305th (Bedfordshire Yeomanry) Medium Regiment RA. This unit was converted to a light regiment in 1955 and amalgamated in 1961 with the Hertfordshire Yeomanry to form 286th (Herts and Beds Yeomanry) Field Regiment RA (qv).

BERKSHIRE

The Berkshire (Hungerford) Yeomanry

The first troop to be raised in Berkshire in 1794 was the Abingdon Troop and it was joined by three further troops in 1804 to form the 1st Berkshire Cavalry which served until 1828. A second regiment, the East Berkshire Yeomanry Cavalry, was formed in 1805 with four troops and served for 22 years. In 1831 the Hungerford Troop was re-raised and a regiment called the Berkshire (Hungerford) Yeomanry Cavalry was subsequently formed. The Regiment provided the 36th Company of the 10th Bn Imperial Yeomanry for service in the South African war.

In the First World War the regiment fought dismounted at Gallipoli and then in the Egyptian and Palestine campaigns as part of the 6th Mounted Brigade. It served briefly in a machine-gun role in Italy and France on amalgamation with the Bucks Yeomanry.

In 1920 the Berkshire Yeomanry was converted to artillery to provide two batteries, 395 and 396 (Berks Yeomanry) Batteries, of 99th (Bucks and Berks Yeomanry) Brigade, RFA. The 'duplicate' unit of 99th Field Regiment, RA, formed in 1939, was 145th (Berkshire Yeomanry) Field Regiment, RA, carrying only the Berkshire Yeomanry title. This Regiment served in Home Forces until 1945 when it moved to India, thence to Malaya and Java.

The Berkshire Yeomanry was re-formed in 1947 as 345th and 346th (Berks Yeomanry) Medium Regiments, RA. These two regiments were amalgamated as 345th Medium Regiment in 1950. The Regiment amalgamated with the Westminster Dragoons in 1961 and in 1967 was reduced to form the Headquarters Squadron of the Royal Yeomanry Regiment. Dividing again in 1982, the successor squadron is 94 (Berkshire Yeomanry) Signal Squadron (Volunteer) which is part of the 71st (Yeomanry) Signal Regiment (V).

BERWICKSHIRE

The Berwickshire Yeomanry Cavalry

The first two troops of Berwickshire Yeomanry Cavalry were raised in 1797 in the Duns district, and a third troop in 1801 in the Eagle district. They served without break and, with the Selkirkshire and Roxburghshire Corps, they exercised at Greenlaw Moor in November 1803. A month later, at the time of the famous

'False Alarm' they turned out almost to a man and proceeded to Dunbar. A fourth troop was raised in Coldstream in 1804. The largest mustered strength of 223 all ranks was recorded in 1827, the year in which the Berwickshire Yeomanry Cavalry was disbanded.

In April 1848 the 3rd or Berwickshire Troop was raised for the East Lothian Yeomanry Cavalry, (see under East Lothian).

BUCKINGHAMSHIRE

The Royal Buckinghamshire Hussars

The first Yeomanry troops in Buckinghamshire, formed in May 1794, were known as the 'Bucks Armed Yeomanry'. After the Peace of Amiens the troops were formed into three regiments, the 1st or Southern Regiment, the 2nd or Mid Bucks Yeomanry Cavalry and the 3rd or Northern Regiment. The 2nd Hussar

An aquatint of the Buckinghamshire Hussars published in 1844, by H. Martens, engraved by J. Harris and published by Fores.

– Royal Green Jackets, Oxford

Regiment of Bucks Yeomanry Cavalry remained in service without pay between 1828–30 while the other two regiments disbanded. (For many years the Taplow troop of the 1st Regiment retained a separate identity until it was disbanded in 1871: in later years it had been equipped for the Lancer role.) The Regiment was designated Buckinghamshire Yeomanry Cavalry (Royal Bucks Hussars) in 1845. During the Boer War the Royal Bucks Hussars provided four companies for the Imperial Yeomanry, Nos 37 and 38 of the 10th Battalion and Nos 56 and 57 of the 15th Battalion.

After service in Egypt the Royal Bucks Hussars left their horses and served as infantry in Gallipoli. Returning to Egypt in 1916, they fought mounted throughout the campaign in Egypt and Palestine, taking part in the mounted action at El Mughar. Amalgamating with the Berkshire Yeomanry as a machine-gun battalion, they served in France in 1918 as C Bn and later 101st Bn, the Machine Gun Corps.

In 1920 the Bucks Yeomanry converted to artillery and formed two Bucks Yeomanry batteries for the 99th (Bucks & Berks) Brigade, RFA. In 1939 this regiment became the 99th (Royal Bucks Yeomanry) Field Regiment and fought in France with 2nd Division in 1940 before being withdrawn at Dunkirk. In 1943 part of the Regiment fought in the Arakan and in 1944 the complete Regiment fought at Kohima and in the Burma Campaign.

In 1947 the 299th (Royal Bucks Yeomanry) Field Regiment, RA(TA) was formed and for two years until 1969 was part of the Buckinghamshire Regiment, RA(T) before being reduced to a cadre and subsequently disbanded.

CAERNARVONSHIRE

In the early 1900s a squadron of the Denbighshire Hussars recruited in Caernarvonshire and included a troop from the Isle of Anglesey. The county name was incorporated in the title of 61st (Caernarvon and Denbigh Yeomanry) Medium Regiment, RA, when it was formed in 1920. (See under Denbighshire.)

CAMBRIDGESHIRE

A corps of Cambridgeshire Yeomanry Cavalry dates from November 1796, and by 1803 there were three troops. In 1831 the Whittlesey and Cambridgeshire Yeomanry was raised and remained in service at least until the 1850s.

CARDIGANSHIRE

A squadron was found by the county for the Pembroke Yeomanry from 1901. (See under Pembrokeshire.)

CARMARTHENSHIRE

The Carmarthenshire Corps of two troops was raised by Lord Dynevor in September 1794, but was disbanded in 1802. It was re-raised in 1814 and served for some years.

From 1901 a squadron was raised in Carmarthenshire for the Pembroke Yeomanry and served until conversion to artillery after the First World War.

CHESHIRE

The Cheshire Yeomanry (Earl of Chester's)

The first troop of Yeomanry Cavalry was raised in Macclesfield in 1797 and a regiment formed in 1803 as the Western Cheshire Volunteer Cavalry, The Earl of Chester's Regiment, later HRH The Prince Regent's Regiment of Cheshire Yeomanry. In 1819 another regiment was raised and the two regiments became known as the 1st and 2nd Regiments, the title substituting 'King's' for 'Prince Regent's' in 1820. The 2nd Regiment disbanded in 1828, but two separate independent troops existed in Stockport (1803–76) and Adlington (1820–38). Infantry companies were briefly incorporated into the 1st Regiment from 1821–4. The Regiment provided two companies for the 2nd Bn, Imperial Yeomanry, the 21st Company, commanded by Lord Arthur Grosvenor (son of the 1st Duke of Westminster), and the 22nd Company.

The Regiment served dismounted in Egypt from 1916. It amalgamated with the Shropshire Yeomanry in 1917, becoming the 10th Bn, The King's Shropshire Light Infantry, and moved to the Western Front in May 1918.

The Earl of Harrington, Honorary Colonel of the Cheshire Yeomanry at the turn of the century, after the practice for the Tent Pegging Competition, open to all Officers in His Majesty's service at the Agricultural Hall, London. His Lordship won the Competition three times, also Post Practice, Tilting at the Ring, Lemon Cutting, Sword v. Sword, Lances v. Sword mounted, Sword v. Sword dismounted – all in one year.

The Regiment retained its cavalry role in 1920 and served until March 1942 in the Middle East as the last but one mounted cavalry regiment of the British Army. It changed role and became 5th Lines of Communications Signals. The Cheshire Yeomanry continued to serve in the Middle East until 1944 when it was re-designated 17th L. of C. Signals (Cheshire Yeomanry) for service in Belgium.

In 1947 the Cheshire Yeomanry re-formed as an armoured regiment and converted to armoured reconnaissance in 1958. On the formation of The Queen's Own Yeomanry, it incorporated 'C' (Cheshire Yeomanry) Squadron as a sabre squadron with an armoured reconnaissance role. A second squadron continues in service as 80 (Cheshire Yeomanry) Signal Squadron (V).

CLACKMANNANSHIRE

Two troops of Clackmannan and Kinross Yeomanry Cavalry are recorded in 1818. There was a proposal to raise a third in that year, but it is not certain whether this occurred.

CORNWALL

During the Years 1794–1838 no less than eighteen troops were raised in Cornwall, the first being the Launceston Troop. From this Troop the North Cornwall Hussars was formed. The Duke of Cornwall's (Loyal Meneage) Yeomanry Cavalry was accepted for service in 1797. The West Penwith Guides, raised in 1803, were accepted as Yeomanry Cavalry in 1805 and became the third of the Cornish regiments, designated the 2nd Cornwall (Penwith) Yeomanry Cavalry.

Fluctuations amongst the troops continued throughout the period, and, seldom being required for aid to the Civil Power, all three regiments were ordered to disband and by 1838 all had disappeared. Cornish squadrons of the 1st Royal Devon Yeomanry existed from time to time, the last being in 1903.

CUMBERLAND

See under Westmorland.

DENBIGHSHIRE

The Denbighshire Hussars

The Wrexham troop of this Regiment was formed in 1795, and the Denbigh Troop in 1799. Two other troops were raised in 1803 and by 1820 five troops existed. The Regiment did not disband in 1828 but served without pay until 1831. For the South African War the Regiment provided the 29th Company of the 9th Bn, Imperial Yeomanry.

In 1916 the Denbighshire Hussars moved to Egypt and served in the Palestine campaign. They became 24th (Denbighshire Yeomanry) Bn, The Royal Welch Fusiliers in 1917 and spent the last six months of the war fighting in France.

An Officer of the Denbighshire Yeomanry Cavalry 1854 by an unknown artist.

– National Army Museum

The Denbighshire Yeomanry was amalgamated with the Caernarvon Royal Garrison Artillery in 1920 to form 61st (Caernarvon and Denbigh Yeomanry) Medium Brigade, RFA, of which two batteries, 241 and 242, were designated as Yeomanry. A 'duplicate' unit, 69th Medium Regiment, RA, was formed in 1939. Both units served with the BEF in 1940 and were evacuated through Dunkirk. Thereafter 61st Medium Regiment served in Home Forces and throughout the campaign in north-west Europe and 69th Medium Regiment in North Africa, fighting at El Alamein and subsequently in the Italian campaign.

The Denbighshire Yeomanry was re-formed in 1947 as 361st (Caernarvon and Denbigh Yeomanry) Medium Regiment, RA, and subsequent changes to 372nd Light and 372nd Field Regiments took place. The Regiment was reduced to a cadre in 1969. The successor unit is B (Flint and Denbighshire Yeomanry) Company, 3rd Volunteer Battalion, The Royal Welch Fusiliers.

DERBYSHIRE

The Derbyshire Yeomanry

Four troops were raised in Derbyshire in 1794 and served until 1828. Only one troop, The Radbourne Troop, remained in service (without pay) during the period until 1830. Two troops were raised in 1831 and 1843, and were regimented in 1864 as the Derbyshire Yeomanry Cavalry. The Derbyshire Yeomanry provided the 8th Company of the 4th Bn, Imperial Yeomanry for the South African war.

As part of the 2nd Mounted Division the Regiment served in Egypt before landing in Gallipoli in August 1915. After further dismounted service in Egypt, the Regiment moved to Macedonia and served there for the rest of the war.

After the war the Derbyshire Yeomanry was reduced and became the 24th Armoured Car Company, RTC. In 1938 two regiments were formed, the 1st and 2nd Derbyshire Yeomanry. The 1st Regiment went to North Africa in November 1942 in the reconnaissance role and were the first British troops to reach Tunis.

Converting to tanks, the Regiment subsequently landed in Italy, fought at Cassino and were the first British troops to reach the River Po and enter Austria. The 2nd Regiment moved to Egypt in 1942 as an armoured reconnaissance regiment and served in the Desert Campaign, taking part in the Battle of El Alamein. After returning to Britain in June 1943, the Regiment landed in Normandy on D plus 1 and fought in the same role through north-west Europe, ending the War at Bremerhaven.

The Derbyshire Yeomanry re-formed in 1947 as an armoured car regiment. In 1956 amalgamation took place, with the Leicestershire Yeomanry (qv).

DEVONSHIRE

The Royal 1st Devon Yeomanry

The Royal 1st Devon Yeomanry Cavalry dates from 1794 when its first troop was raised. It became regimented in 1801 and received its 'Royal' title in 1803 due to its services in aid of the Civil Power. It continued serving without pay from 1828 until 1831 and has never been disbanded. The Royal 1st Devon Yeomanry provided the 26th Company of the 7th Bn, Imperial Yeomanry, for the South African war.

After mobilisation in 1914 the Regiment served in the Home Forces until being sent to Gallipoli in October 1915. It was withdrawn to Egypt at the end of the year and was tasked throughout 1916 with mounted and dismounted patrolling and Suez Canal defence. In 1916 the amalgamation took place with the Royal North Devon Hussars, forming the 16th Bn, The Devonshire Regiment. It fought as infantry as part of the 74th (Yeomanry) Division, (known as the 'Broken Spur' Division), through Egypt and Palestine until moving to the Western Front in May 1918.

The Royal 1st Devon Yeomanry and the Royal North Devon Yeomanry were amalgamated in 1920 and converted to artillery to form 96th (Devonshire Yeomanry) Brigade, RFA. The title 'Royal' was restored in 1923 and it became known as the Royal Devon Yeomanry Artillery. In 1939 a 'duplicate' unit, 142nd

Royal 1st Devon Yeomanry, machine gun section c1910.
– Royal Devon Yeomanry

(Royal Devon Yeomanry) Field Regiment was raised. 96th Field Regiment served in the Home Forces, moving to India in January 1945, while 142nd Field Regiment fought in Sicily from July 1942 and Italy.

In 1947 both regiments were re-formed, as 296th Field Regiment, RA, and 342nd Medium Regiment, RA, both designated 'Royal Devon Yeomanry'. The two were amalgamated in 1950 as 296th Field Regiment which survived until 1967. The successor squadron, D (Royal Devon Yeomanry) Squadron, forms a sabre squadron of the Royal Wessex Yeomanry in the home defence reconnaissance role.

The Royal North Devon Hussars

The first troop of this Regiment dates from 1798 and it was regimented with other troops in 1803. Serving without pay from 1828–31, the Regiment was never disbanded. During the South African war it provided the 27th (Royal North Devon) Company, the 7th Bn, Imperial Yeomanry with the Royal 1st Devon company.

After service in Home Forces cavalry during the Great War, the Regiment sailed for Gallipoli to fight as infantry. Amalgamation with the Royal 1st Devon Yeomanry took place in Egypt in 1916. After the war the Regiment again amalgamated with the Royal 1st Devon Yeomanry (qv).

DORSET

The Queen's Own Dorset Yeomanry

The first corps in Dorset was raised in 1794 but lapsed after the Treaty of Amiens. It was re-raised in 1803, disbanded in 1814 and accepted for service for the third time in 1830 as a county regiment, independent troops having served at various times. The Dorset Yeomanry provided an element of the 7th Bn, Imperial Yeomanry, for the Boer War with the Devon and Somerset companies.

Mobilised in 1914 the Regiment proceeded to Egypt and in August 1915 landed in Gallipoli with the 2nd (South Midlands) Mounted Brigade. Returning to Egypt in 1916 it became part of the 6th Mounted Brigade and served throughout the Palestine campaign.

The Dorset Yeomanry was amalgamated with the West Somerset Yeomanry and the Somerset Royal Horse Artillery in 1920 to form 94th (Dorset and Somerset Yeomanry) Brigade, RFA, in which 375 and 376 Batteries were designated 'Dorset Yeomanry'. In 1929 94th Brigade was reorganised entirely within Dorset and with the title 'Dorset Yeomanry'. The additional title 'Queen's Own' was restored in 1930. 94th Field Regiment fought with 43rd (Wessex) Infantry Division throughout the campaign in north-west Europe from June 1944, and was heavily involved in the fighting near Caen. The 'duplicate' regiment, 141st Field Regiment, remained with Home Forces.

The 'Queen's Own Dorset Yeomanry' title was carried into the post-war Territorial Army by 294th Field Regiment, RA, and 341st Medium Regiment, RA. These two regiments were amalgamated as 294th Field Regiment in 1950. In 1961 the Dorset Yeomanry became 250th Medium Regiment with the West Somerset Yeomanry and, in 1967, was absorbed into the infantry. The successor unit is 'D' Company (Queen's Own Dorset Yeomanry), 1st Bn, the Wessex Volunteers.

DUMFRIESSHIRE

In 1798 a corps of Yeomanry Cavalry was raised for Dumfriess, and by 1803, a second troop was in being. Later there were five troops in existence and they served until the 1820s.

DUNBARTONSHIRE

Little is known of the Yeomanry Cavalry in Dunbartonshire. There were two separate corps in 1803 which, by the year 1820, had risen to three.

DURHAM

A corps of Yeomanry Cavalry was raised in North Durham in 1798, and in 1801 a second troop was raised in the city of Durham. By 1803 there were twelve troops in the county, but they do not appear to have been regimented. Some were still serving in the 1820s.

ESSEX

The Essex Yeomanry

The Essex Yeomanry was not regimented until 1813 when six previously independent troops formed the 1st Essex Yeomanry Cavalry. It was disbanded in 1828 but reformed as the West Essex Yeomanry Cavalry in 1830. It served without pay for five years from 1838 and was disbanded in 1877. An Essex Troop served with the Loyal Suffolk Hussars for a number of years.

An Essex yeoman c1902 having just won the 'Smartness on Parade' prize. Trooper Wallis of the Brentwood Troop.

– Essex Yeomanry

The Regiment was re-raised in 1901. In 1914 it was sent to France and served on the Western Front, retaining its horses throughout. In April 1918 the Regiment was divided, and the three squadrons were attached to regular cavalry regiments for the remainder of the war.

The Essex Yeomanry trained as cavalry for nearly two years after they were re-formed in 1920, but in November 1921 they became artillery as the two-battery 104th (Essex Yeomanry) Brigade, RFA. A third battery formed from the old Essex Royal Horse Artillery joined the brigade in 1932 and the Regiment's name subsequently included 'RHA'. The 'duplicate' unit, 147th Field Regiment, was formed in 1939. 104th Regiment, RHA, served in Palestine with 1st Cavalry Division, then throughout the campaign in North Africa, including fighting at the Battle of El Alamein. It subsequently fought in the campaign in Italy.

In 1942 414 Battery was detached from 104th Regiment to serve as an independent battery in Burma and formed the basis for expansion into a new regiment, 14th Regiment, RHA. 147th Field Regiment served in Home Forces and then landed on D-Day to fight throughout the north-west Europe campaign. A fourth regiment, 191st (Herts and Essex Yeomanry) Field Regiment, RA, was formed in 1942 with cadres provided by 147th Field Regiment and the Hertfordshire Yeomanry (qv). It fought in north-west Europe.

The Essex Yeomanry was represented in the post-war TA by 304th (Essex Yeomanry, RHA) Field Regiment, RA, which served until 1967. After a short period as a cadre it was converted to Royal Signals in 1969 as 70 (Essex Yeomanry) Signal Squadron (V).

FIFE

The Fife and Forfar Yeomanry

The Kirkcaldy Troop was formed in 1797. It continued service through 1802 and amalgamated with the Fife Yeomanry Cavalry in 1803. Disbanded in 1828, re-raised in 1831, it survived until 1838. In 1860 the Fife Volunteer Mounted Rifles were raised and later designated Fife Light Horse. In 1901 it amalgamated with the Forfar Light Horse. Together they provided the 20th Company of the 6th Bn, Imperial Yeomanry for service in South Africa.

The Regiment landed in Gallipoli in September 1915 and served on the peninsula until it was withdrawn to Egypt, to serve on Canal defences in 1916. After being redesignated 14th (Fife and Forfar Yeomanry) Bn, The Black Watch, it fought in the Palestine Campaign. In May 1918, the Battalion landed in France and served on the Western front until the end of the war.

Between the wars the Fife and Forfar Yeomanry served as the 20th Armoured Car Company, Royal Tank Corps. Rapidly expanding in 1939, two divisional cavalry regiments were formed. (They were equipped with light tanks and bren-gun carriers for the reconnaissance role.) The First Regiment went to France with the 51st Highland Division in January 1940 and came out through Dunkirk. Both regiments became armoured regiments in 9th Armoured and 11th Armoured Divisions respectively. The 2nd Fife and Forfar Yeomanry landed in Normandy on 17 June, 1944 and was involved in much fighting during the following campaign, ending the war at Lübeck on the Baltic. During the summer of 1944 the 1st Regiment re-equipped with flame-throwing tanks and, as part of the 79th Armoured Division, fought in north-west Europe from the autumn of that year. The Regiment was preparing to go to South East Asia when the war ended.

The Fife and Forfar Yeomanry was re-formed as an armoured car regiment in 1947. Amalgamation with the Scottish Horse followed in 1956 and the successor unit served as 239 (Highland Yeomanry) Squadron, RCT(V). In 1992 they formed C Squadron of the Scottish Yeomanry.

FLINTSHIRE

The Flintshire Yeomanry Cavalry

This Corps was raised in 1831 by Lord George Grosvenor. It was only in existence for seven years but found four well-recruited troops at Eaton Hall, Mold, Hawarden and Holywell.

The county name re-appeared in 1967 connected with the Denbighshire Yeomanry (qv) serving as Royal Artillery.

GLAMORGANSHIRE

The Glamorgan Yeomanry

The Glamorgan Yeomanry Cavalry was raised in 1797, three separate corps being recorded, and served until 1831. They were heavily involved in the Merthyr Tydfil riots in that year, but all three corps were disbanded soon afterwards.

The Glamorganshire Imperial Yeomanry were raised in 1901 with three squadrons, the fourth being formed a year later. During the Great War, the Regiment went to Egypt in 1916 and fought dismounted. It was amalgamated a year later and became 24th (Pembroke and Glamorgan) Bn, The Welch Regiment, for action in the Palestine Campaign, and in 1918 on the Western Front.

The Glamorganshire Yeomanry was converted to artillery in 1920 and reduced to a sub-unit as 324 (Glamorgan Yeomanry) Battery, 81st (Welsh) Brigade, RFA. In 1939 324 Field Battery was re-regimented into the 'duplicate' unit of 81st Field Regiment – 132nd (Welsh) Field Regiment. 324 Field Battery served in Home Forces until crossing to Normandy late in June 1944, after which it took part in the campaign in north-west Europe.

The Glamorgan Yeomanry title was not officially included in the post-war Territorial Army but was in fact carried by a battery of 281st (Welsh) Field Regiment, RA, later absorbed into 282nd (Glamorgan and Monmouthshire) Field Regiment, RA. The successors are C Troop, 211 (Glamorgan Yeomanry) Air Defence Battery, RA(V).

GLOUCESTERSHIRE

The Royal Gloucestershire Hussars

The first troop was formed in Cheltenham in 1795 and, like a number of other troops in the county, remained independent until disbandment in 1827. A new troop was raised in 1831 and the Regiment was formed in 1834 by the Marquis of Worcester, heir to the Duke of Beaufort. (Successive members of the Somerset family have served continuously for 150 years and apart from a 13 years' gap, have

This unusual photograph shows a detachment of the Royal Gloucestershire Hussars in full dress at the Schloss Schonbraun Tattoo in Austria during the period of occupation after the Second World War.

– Royal Gloucestershire Hussars

always been Colonels or Honorary Colonels.) The Regiment provided the 3rd Company of the First Battalion of the Imperial Yeomanry in the Boer War and served for eighteen months in South Africa.

The Royal Gloucestershire Hussars went first to Egypt during the First World War and subsequently fought dismounted at Gallipoli in 1915, before returning to Egypt and the defence of the Suez Canal. The Regiment fought as cavalry during the Palestine campaign and ended the war in Syria.

The RGH spent the inter-war years reduced to squadron strength as the 21st (Royal Gloucestershire Hussars) Armoured Car Company, RTC, and at the outbreak of the Second World War it was reconstituted as an armoured regiment before becoming a training regiment of the RAC. The 2nd RGH was raised in 1939 and equipped with tanks. It formed part of 22nd Armoured Brigade and fought in the Western Desert from late in 1941, sustaining overwhelming casualties. Some of the members of the Regiment fought at Alamein. The 2nd

RGH was not fully reconstituted, but 1st RGH served at the end of the war as garrison troops in Austria.

After the war, the Regiment formed an armoured car regiment, but was reduced in 1969 to a cadre. At the present date the Royal Gloucestershire Hussars are represented by A and HQ Squadrons and the Band of the Royal Wessex Yeomanry.

HAMPSHIRE

The Hampshire Carabiniers

In 1794 the North Hampshire Yeomanry Cavalry was accepted and reached a strength of three troops. Suffering disbandment in 1828, it was re-formed in 1830 but later lost its 'North' prefix. A troop of Yeomanry existed on the Isle of Wight for many years. The Regiment adopted the title 'Carabiniers' in 1884 and formed the 41st Company of the 4th Bn, Imperial Yeomanry, and 50th Company of the 17th Bn, Imperial Yeomanry, for the South African war.

Remaining in England until 1916, the squadrons were sent separately to France. RHQ & B Squadron formed IX Corps Cavalry Regiment in France. The Regiment was re-united in 1917 and at the end of that year was converted to infantry, forming 15th (Hampshire Yeomanry) Bn, The Hampshire Regiment. It served for four months in Italy before returning to the Western Front.

The Hampshire Yeomanry was amalgamated with the Hampshire Royal Horse Artillery in 1920 to form a two-battery army brigade, 95th (Hampshire Yeomanry) Brigade, RFA. In 1938 the Regiment was converted to the anti-aircraft role and mobilised in 1939 as 72nd (Hampshire) Heavy Anti-Aircraft Regiment, RA, in which one battery, 217 HAA Battery, was designated 'Hampshire Carabiniers'. The Regiment served in Air Defence, Great Britain until November 1942 when it landed in North Africa. It later served in Italy.

In 1947 the Hampshire Yeomanry was re-formed as 295th (Hampshire Carabiniers) HAA Regiment, RA. After further amalgamation the title was lost in 1967, but is now held by 227 (Hampshire Yeomanry) Amphibious Field Squadron RE.

HEREFORDSHIRE

A Hereford corps of Yeomanry Cavalry was raised in 1803 and was still serving in the 1820s.

HERTFORDSHIRE

The Hertfordshire Yeomanry

Five independent troops of Yeomanry Cavalry were raised in Hertfordshire in June 1794. One by one they disbanded between 1807 and 1824. In late 1830 and early 1831 seven new troops were formed, four of which were grouped as the South Hertfordshire Corps. Of the three independent troops, only the North Hertfordshire troop survived and it amalgamated with the South Hertfordshire Corps to form the Hertfordshire Yeomanry Cavalry in 1871. The 42nd (Hertfordshire) Company, 12th Bn, Imperial Yeomanry, was formed by the

Regiment, serving in South Africa from March 1900 to May 1901.

On mobilisation in 1914, the Hertfordshire Yeomanry sailed almost immediately for garrison duty in Egypt. The Regiment served dismounted in Gallipoli from August to November 1915. Re-mounted, it took part in the campaign against the Senussi on the Western Frontier before being broken up, the three squadrons being attached to infantry divisions. D Squadron spent the rest of the war in Mesopotamia, while A and B Squadrons served mainly in Egypt and Palestine. In the final stages of the campaign they were part of the XXI Corps Cavalry Regiment.

In 1920 the Hertfordshire Yeomanry was amalgamated with the two Hertfordshire batteries of RFA to form 86th (East Anglian) (Herts Yeomanry) Brigade, RFA. Re-designated in 1938 as 86th Field Regiment, it was 'duplicated' in 1939 to form in addition 135th Field Regiment, RA. In 1938 another regiment, 79th (Herts Yeomanry) Heavy Anti-Aircraft Regiment, RA, was formed. 86th Field Regiment served in Home Forces until landing on D-Day in Normandy and fighting for the rest of the War in north-west Europe.

135th Field Regiment fought in Malaya and Singapore and was captured after the fall of Singapore. After service with the BEF in 1940, 79th Heavy Anti-Aircraft Regiment served later in North Africa and Italy. A fourth regiment, formed in 1942, was 191st (Herts and Essex Yeomanry) Field Regiment, RA. It fought in France, Belgium and Holland.

In 1947 two regiments were re-formed. 286th Field Regiment and 479th HAA Regiment, both designated 'Herts Yeomanry'. They were amalgamated in 1955 and, in 1961, 286th (Herts Yeomanry) Field Regiment, RA, was amalgamated with 305th (Bedfordshire Yeomanry) Light Regiment, RA, as 286th (Herts and Beds Yeomanry) Field Regiment, RA. The successor unit is 201st (Herts and Beds Yeomanry) Field Battery, RA(V).

HUNTINGDONSHIRE

A corps of Yeomanry Cavalry was commissioned for the county in April 1794. Three troops are recorded in 1803 and appear to have served until the 1820s.

In 1860 the Huntingdonshire Mounted Rifles (The Duke of Manchester's Light Horse) were raised, with two troops in Bedfordshire. It was disbanded in 1882.

INVERNESS-SHIRE

The Lovat Scouts

Lord Lovat (formerly of the 1st Life Guards) raised two Companies of 'scouts', one mounted and one dismounted, for service in South Africa. The men were mainly stalkers and ghillies from the Highlands. In 1901 the second contingent of Lovat Scouts were designated Imperial Yeomanry and formed the 99th and 100th Companies.

Two regiments of Lovat Scouts were authorised in 1903 as Yeomanry. Both served dismounted in Gallipoli and withdrew to Egypt. In September 1916 they became nominally the 10th (Lovat Scouts) Bn, the Queen's Own Cameron Highlanders, and were embarked for service in Macedonia on the Bulgarian front. Detachments served as observers in France from late 1916.

Lovat Scouts pose to be photographed in South Africa. They are wearing the pith helmet as opposed to the familiar slouch hat associated with this battalion.

– Lovat Scouts Museum

Between the wars the Regiment served in a special 'scouts' role, retaining a proportion of horses, which suited their traditional skills in mountainous terrain. In 1940 the Scouts moved as infantry to the Faroe Islands to counter the threat of German occupation. They then became a mountain recce regiment, after suitable mountain training in Canada, and served in Italy from July 1944, mainly as special patrol troops.

In 1947 the Lovat Scouts were reduced in strength, transferred to the RAC and incorporated in the Scottish Horse (qv) as C Squadron. This was a short-lived arrangement, for they soon became an independent mountain battery of the Royal Artillery, 850 Mountain Battery. The battery was expanded to form 677th (Lovat Scouts) Mountain Regiment, RA, in 1949 and the title was carried on by 540th Light Anti-Aircraft Regiment, RA, after extensive reorganisation in 1950. This regiment served until 1967 when the title was adopted by an infantry company. The successors now serve in two companies of the 2nd Bn, 51st Highland Volunteers, TA, A (Queen's Own Highlanders and Lovat Scouts) Company and D (Gordons and Lovat Scouts) Company, recruiting in Orkney and Shetland.

KENT

The Royal East Kent Mounted Rifles (Duke of Connaught's Own)

Independent troops of Yeomanry were commissioned in 1794, partly regimented in 1803 and were fully regimented in 1813. The Regiment disbanded in 1828 but was the first to offer to re-form in 1830. In 1853 they were redesignated 'Mounted Rifles' and later became the Duke of Connaught's Own Royal East Kent Mounted Rifles. The Regiment provided the 33rd Company of the 11th Battalion for the South African war.

After serving in Home Defence, the Regiment sailed direct to Gallipoli in October 1915. Withdrawing from the peninsula, the REKMR provided two sub-units for a composite regiment with the Queen's Own West Kent Yeomanry. They were used to defend the Suez Canal and took part as dismounted infantry, in the Palestine campaign. Redesignated as the 10th Bn, The Buffs, the Regiment served in France for the last six months of the war.

The Royal East Kent Yeomanry and the West Kent Yeomanry were amalgamated in 1920 and converted to artillery as 97th (Kent Yeomanry) Brigade, RFA. Within this brigade two batteries, 385 and 386, were designated 'Duke of Connaught's Own Yeomanry' and two, 387 and 388, 'Queen's Own Yeomanry'. When the 'duplicate' unit, 143rd Field Regiment, RA, was formed in 1939, it continued the custom of constituent batteries from both East and West Kent. 97th Field Regiment served in France and Belgium with the BEF. After a period in Home Forces the regiment moved to Iraq, then to North Africa, where it fought at the Battle of El Alamein. Subsequently the Regiment fought in the campaign in Italy. 143rd Field Regiment served in Home Forces until June 1944, and then throughout the campaign in north-west Eurpoe.

The Kent Yeomanry was reconstituted in 1947 as the 297th Light Anti-Aircraft Regiment, RA. In 1961 the Kent Yeomanry amalgamated with the 3/4 County of London Yeomanry (Sharpshooters) to form the Kent and County of London Yeomanry (Sharpshooters), an armoured reconnaissance regiment. The successor units are C (Kent and Sharpshooters Yeomanry) Squadron of the Royal Yeomanry and HQ and 265 (Kent and Sharpshooters Yeomanry) Signal Squadrons (V).

The Queen's Own West Kent Yeomanry

The Regiment was formed in 1797 from troops which had been in existence since the inception of the Yeomanry Cavalry in 1794. Disbanded in 1827, it was restored again in 1831 (the Chislehurst troop having been raised in 1830) and continued to serve throughout the nineteenth century. A company was found by

This period piece of 1903 shows the Main Gate Guard at Cobham Park, Kent during the annual camp of the Queen's Own West Kent Yeomanry.

– Kent and Sharpshooters Yeomanry

the Regiment for the South African war and designated 36th Company of the 11th Battalion.

The history of the Queen's Own West Kent Yeomanry during the First World War is identical to that of the Royal East Kent Mounted Rifles. They were amalgamated in 1920 and their subsequent history can be seen above.

KINROSS

See under Clackmannan.

KIRKCUDBRIGHTSHIRE

Three troops of Yeomanry Cavalry were raised in the county in 1803 and served until 1826. In 1831 a corps was re-raised but soon disappeared.

LANARKSHIRE

The Lanarkshire Yeomanry

Three troops of Yeomanry were raised in the Upper Ward of Lanarkshire in 1819 and, by 1867, three more had been formed. The Regiment was kept in service without a break and were often called out in aid of the Civil Power, indeed in 1856 it was on permanent duty for six weeks. For the South African war the regiment provided the 17th Company of the 6th Bn, Imperial Yeomanry, with the Ayrshire Company.

The Regiment was sent to Gallipoli in 1915 and fought there dismounted. It then moved to Egypt. In 1917 it amalgamated to form the 12th (Ayr and Lanark Yeomanry) Bn, The Royal Scots Fusiliers, and, after service in Palestine, moved to France for the last five months of the war.

The Lanarkshire Yeomanry was re-formed as a cavalry regiment after the war and retained the role until 1940 when it was divided to form 155th and 156th Field Regiments, RA. 155th (Lanarkshire Yeomanry) Field Regiment was sent to India in May 1941 and subsequently to Malaya in September 1941, where it was lost in the Japanese invasion. One of the batteries of the Regiment had been previously moved to join 160th Field Regiment which served in the Arakan Operation in 1943 and in Burma in 1945. 156th (Lanarkshire Yeomanry) Field Regiment served in Persia, Syria, Egypt, Sicily and Italy, returning to Egypt and Palestine in 1944.

Re-formed in 1947 as an armoured regiment, the Lanarkshire Yeomanry subsequently amalgamated with the other Lowland regiments to form the Queen's Own Lowland Yeomanry, which ceased to exist as a regiment by 1969. The successor unit was 225 (Queen's Own Lowland Yeomanry) Squadron, RCT(V) until 1992, when it re-formed as the Lanarkshire and Glasgow Yeomanry Squadron of the Scottish Yeomanry.

The Queen's Own Royal Glasgow Yeomanry

Troops were raised in the Glasgow area at various times from 1797 and there was a connection with the Royal Glasgow Light Horse, which dated from 1796, and the Glasgow Sharpshooters. After disbandment in 1802, various corps were re-raised

Officers of The Queen's Own Glasgow Yeomanry c1890.

– Major J. C. K. Young

only to be disbanded in 1814 and 1828. The Glasgow Troop, it is claimed, was never formally disbanded. A regiment was raised in 1848 and became known as The Queen's Own Royal Glasgow and Lower Ward of Lanarkshire Yeomanry until 1914. For the South African war the Regiment provided the 18th Company of the 6th Bn, Imperial Yeomanry.

In 1915 the Regiment was divided, squadrons joining various formations in France and Flanders. A and B Squadrons were reunited in 1916 in the V Corps Cavalry Regiment and a year later were dismounted, finally ending the war as 18th (Royal Glasgow Yeomanry) Bn, The Highland Light Infantry. RHQ and C Squadrons served in Egypt and Gallipoli and served, mounted, in the Palestine campaign.

In 1920 the Queen's Own Royal Glasgow Yeomanry was converted to artillery to form a two-battery Army Brigade, 101st (QORGY) Brigade, RFA. On conversion to the anti-tank role in 1939, 101st Field Regiment became 54th (QORGY) Anti-Tank Regiment. The new regiment incorporated two additional batteries, 215 and 216, which did not carry the Yeomanry title. The 'duplicate' regiment was 64th (QORGY) Anti-Tank Regiment, RA. The 54th Regiment served briefly in France in 1940 and one of the batteries served in Singapore before its capture by the Japanese. Other batteries landed in north-west Europe in 1944. The 64th Regiment served in the Western Desert, Sicily and Italy.

In 1947 the Glasgow Yeomanry was reconstituted as an armoured regiment, but merged in 1956 with the Lanarkshire Yeomanry.

LANCASHIRE

The Duke of Lancaster's Own Yeomanry

The first troop of this regiment was the Bolton Troop, which dated from April 1798 and continued in service until 1814. The Furness Troop was raised in 1819 and in 1828 it was joined by the Bolton and Wigan Troop to form the Lancashire

Regiment of Yeomanry cavalry, renamed in 1834 the Duke of Lancaster's Own Yeomanry Cavalry after their Colonel-in-Chief, the Sovereign. The Regiment formed the 23rd Company of the 8th Bn, Imperial Yeomanry for service in South Africa.

During the Great War the Regiment was split. A Squadron served in the Middle East guarding the Canal, fighting the Senussi in Egypt and joining the Palestine campaign as divisional cavalry. The remainder of the Regiment served separately as divisional cavalry at first, then regimented as a corps cavalry regiment. It ended the War as an infantry battalion, the 12th (DLOY) Bn, The Manchester Regiment.

The Duke of Lancaster's Own Yeomanry retained its horses between the wars and was mobilised as a mounted regiment in 1939. In August 1940 the Regiment was converted to artillery and formed 77th and 78th (DLOY) Medium Regiments, RA. 77th Medium Regiment landed in Normandy in June 1944 and took part in the campaign in north-west Europe. 78th Medium Regiment remained at home until it moved to the Middle East and fought at El Alamein. Later it landed in Italy and served there until the close of the campaign.

In 1947 the regiment re-formed first as a divisional regiment, then a reconnaissance regiment of the RAC. It amalgamated with the 40/41st Royal Tank Regiment in 1967. Reduced to a cadre in 1969, the DLOY re-formed as an infantry regiment in 1971. The Duke of Lancaster's Own Yeomanry fulfils a light reconnaissance role as D Squadron, Royal Mercian and Lancastrian Yeomanry.

The Lancashire Hussars

The Ashton Yeomanry Cavalry was commissioned in 1798 and served until 1823. In 1848 a new Regiment was formed from those who were serving in the Duke of Lancaster's Own Yeomanry Cavalry. It was mainly comprised of Roman Catholics and was commanded by Sir John Gerard (whose family had raised the original Ashton Troop). The Regiment provided volunteers to fight in South Africa by forming the 32nd Company of the 2nd Bn, Imperial Yeomanry, the 77th Company of the 8th Bn and part of 23rd company with the DLOY.

During the First World War, the Regiment was divided, sending D Squadron to France as cavalry in 1915, and C Squadron in 1916, forming together the 8th Corps Cavalry. Later they reorganised as the 18th (Lancashire Hussars) Bn, The King's Liverpool Regiment. Two other squadrons served in the Middle East from 1915.

The Regiment was converted to artillery after the war as 106 (Lancashire Yeomanry) Army Brigade, RFA. In 1938 it became 106th Regiment, RHA. In March 1941 it became 106th Light Anti-Aircraft Regiment, RHA, which disbanded in July of that year, the second Regiment having been formed in March 1939 as 149th (Lancashire Yeomanry) Regiment, RHA. It served in Egypt and the Western Desert as 149 Anti-Tank Regiment (1941) and moved to Italy in December 1943. A year later the batteries were separated and sent to various parts of Greece for the remainder of the war.

In 1947 the Lancashire Hussars re-formed as two regiments, 349 Light Anti-Aircraft and 306 Heavy Anti-Aircraft Regiments. Successive changes in designation have followed and the Lancashire Hussars were subsequently absorbed into the Lancashire Artillery.

LEICESTERSHIRE

The Leicestershire Yeomanry (Prince Albert's Own)

The Leicestershire Light Horse was raised in 1794 but disbanded in 1802. Re-raised in 1803 they have served continuously since that date. During the South African war the Regiment provided two companies, the 7th Company of the 11th Bn, Imperial Yeomanry and the 65th Company of the 17th Bn.

From November 1914 the Leicestershire Yeomanry served as a mounted regiment in France and Flanders. It was briefly dismounted in early 1918 and trained with the North Somerset Yeomanry as a machine-gun battalion, but was restored to its cavalry role and the squadrons attached for the rest of the war to regular regiments.

The Leicestershire Yeomanry remained a mounted regiment between the wars and was mobilised as such in 1939. In August 1940 the regiment was converted to artillery and formed 153rd and 154th (Leicestershire Yeomanry) Field Regiments, RA. 153rd Field Regiment became part of the divisional artillery of the newly formed Guards Armoured Division and fought with the Division throughout the campaign in north-west Europe. 154th Field Regiment served in Palestine and Syria and then in North Africa, including the Battle of El Alamein. In 1944 it moved to Italy and fought there until the close of the campaign.

They served as B (Leicestershire and Derbyshire Yeomanry) Company of the 3rd (Volunteer) Bn, The Worcestershire and Sherwood Foresters Regiment (29th/45th Foot), and a company of 7th Volunteer Bn, The Royal Anglian Regiment, known as the Leicestershire and Derbyshire Yeomanry (Prince Albert's Own) Company, until re-forming as B Squadron the Royal Yeomanry.

LINCOLNSHIRE

The Lincolnshire Yeomanry

Independent troops were raised in Lincolnshire from 1794 and served until 1828. The Lincoln Light Horse comprised four troops and a further ten existed. Re-raised in 1831, the North Lincoln Regiment of Yeomanry Cavalry served until 1846 when it was disbanded.

The Lincolnshire Yeomanry was raised in May 1901. After mobilisation in 1914, it remained in England until 1915 and then moved to Egypt. It subsequently took part mounted in the Palestine campaign. In 1918 the Regiment joined the 1/1st East Riding Yeomanry to form D Battalion, The Machine Gun Corps, for service in France for the last five months of the war. It was disbanded in 1920.

LONDON

The City of London Yeomanry (The Rough Riders)

This Regiment claims descent from the Loyal Islington Troop of 1798, which was disbanded in 1802 and re-raised in 1803. It became the Loyal London Volunteer Cavalry but disbanded in 1814.

In December 1899 a battalion of 'Rough Riders' was raised for service in South

Africa. Numbered the 20th Battalion, (it drew its name from Colonel Theodore Roosevelt's volunteer cavalry in Cuba), it fought with distinction in the war. Returning members of the Regiment formed in 1901 the 1st County of London Imperial Yeomanry (Rough Riders), subsequently redesignated 'City of London'.

During the First World War the Regiment moved to Egypt and thence, dismounted, to Gallipoli in August 1915. Resuming a cavalry role it served in Egypt, Salonika and Palestine, before amalgamating with the Sharpshooters to form E Battalion, The Machine Gun Corps, for service in France.

In 1920 the City of London Yeomanry was converted to artillery and formed, at first C Battery, then No 1 (City of London Yeomanry) Battery in 11 (HAC and City of London Yeomanry) Brigade, RHA. Later the Battery was detached from the Brigade to provide the basis for expansion to 11th Light Anti-Aircraft Regiment, RA (City of London Yeomanry) (Rough Riders). The Regiment served in the Western Desert from November 1942. A year later it moved to Italy and, widely dispersed, served both as anti-aircraft gunners and infantry.

The Rough Riders re-formed as an armoured regiment in 1947 and in 1961 amalgamated with the Inns of Court Regiment to form the Inns of Court and City Yeomanry. The successors are now the 68 (Inns of Court and City Yeomanry) Signal Squadron (Volunteers) and the band of the Royal Yeomanry.

The Inns of Court Regiment

The Inns of Court first raised a volunteer corps in 1584 and the descent to modern times has been continuous. The Regiment was the 14th Middlesex (Inns of Court) Rifle Volunteers prior to the formation of the Territorial Force in 1908. Given an 'officer producing' role, it became the Inns of Court Officers' Training Corps. As such it served throughout the 1914–18 War and for the greater part of the inter-war period. It became the Inns of Court Regiment in 1932 and continued to train officers for the cavalry and infantry. In 1937 it was listed as 'Cavalry, Territorial Army' and comprised one cavalry and two tank squadrons.

Shortly after mobilisation in the Second World War it was transferred to the Royal Armoured Corps as an armoured car regiment. One squadron landed in Normandy on D-Day and the Regiment fought throughout the campaign in north-west Europe.

After the War, the Regiment was retained as an armoured car regiment, RAC, and for a time was joined by a squadron of the Northamptonshire Yeomanry in 1956, (although the Inns of Court Regiment was still not officially designated Yeomanry). In 1961 it amalgamated with the City of London Yeomanry (qv) to form the Inns of Court and City Yeomanry.

The 1st County of London Yeomanry (Middlesex, Duke of Cambridge's Hussars)

The Uxbridge Troop was raised in 1797 but disbanded in 1802. In 1830 the Troop was re-raised and in 1838 became the Middlesex Yeomanry Cavalry, and as the Metropolis expanded, took recruits from many parts of the county of Middlesex. It provided three companies for service in South Africa, the 34th and 35th companies of the 11th Bn, Imperial Yeomanry and 62nd Company of the 14th Bn. In 1908 it became the 1st County of London Yeomanry (Middlesex Yeomanry Hussars), the title of 1st CLY having formerly been held by the Rough Riders.

Mobilised in 1914, the Regiment moved to Egypt in early 1915. In August 1915 the Middlesex Yeomanry left Egypt for service in the Gallipoli campaign Returning to Egypt, the Regiment later spent six months in Macedonia and then, as part of 5 Mounted Brigade, took part in the Palestine and Syrian campaigns.

In 1920 the Middlesex Hussars were reconstituted and converted to signals as 2nd Cavalry Divisional Signals, and in 1938 the Regiment became Mobile Divisional Signals. A year later the Regiment was 'duplicated'. The 1st Cavalry Divisional Signals (Middlesex Yeomanry) went to the Middle East and served in Syria, Iraq, Tobruk and Crete. On mechanisation, squadrons were formed for 10th Armoured Division, and the squadron with 9 Armoured Brigade served at El Alamein and later in Italy. The duplicate regiment, 2nd Armoured Divisional Signals (Middlesex Yeomanry) also served in the Western Desert and Greece. Some elements of Middlesex Yeomanry served with Special Forces.

On the reconstitution of the Territorial Army in 1947, the Middlesex Hussars became 16th Airborne Division Signals. Subsequently they became 40th Signal Regiment and in 1961 amalgamated with the 47th (London) Signal Regiment which was redesignated 47th (Middlesex Yeomanry) Signal Regiment. The successor sub-unit is 47 (Middlesex Yeomanry) Signal Squadron (V), and a band.

The 2nd County of London Yeomanry (Westminster Dragoons)

The Westminster Volunteer Cavalry was raised in 1797. (It had no direct connection with the renowned London and Westminster Light Horse Volunteers). It served until disbandment in 1802. The 2nd County of London Imperial Yeomanry (Westminster Dragoons) was formed in 1901 with a nucleus of South African War veterans.

The Westminster Dragoons were already serving mounted in Egypt when they were sent dismounted to Gallipoli in August 1915. After the withdrawal from the peninsula the Regiment regained its horses and fought in Egypt and Palestine. In 1918 it was transferred to the Machine Gun Corps, forming first F Battalion and then 104th Battalion, and served in France from August 1918 to the end of the War. Elements of the 2/2nd County of London Yeomanry, it is believed, served for a time in France.

In 1920 the Regiment was transferred to the Tank Corps as 22nd (London) Armoured Car Company (Westminster Dragoons) and it became the principal 'officer producing' source for the Royal Tank Corps (TA). In 1938 it was expanded to become the 22nd Bn RTC (Westminster Dragoons) and, on the outbreak of war, became 102nd Officer Cadet Training Unit. In November 1940 it converted to an armoured regiment of the RAC regaining its full title. It was later issued with flail tanks and landed in Normandy on D-Day and fought throughout the campaign in north-west Europe.

The Regiment re-formed in 1947 as an armoured regiment. It amalgamated in 1961 with the Berkshire Yeomanry and converted to armoured cars. In 1967 the Regiment was reduced and provided the Headquarters Squadron for the Royal Yeomanry Regiment (the title was subsequently altered to The Royal Yeomanry). The current title is HQ (Westminster Dragoons) Squadron.

The 3rd County of London Yeomanry (The Sharpshooters)

Three Sharpshooters' battalions were raised in early 1900 and formed the 18th, 21st and 23rd battalions of the Imperial Yeomanry. Their members were selected from a large number of applicants who could prove their skill with the rifle as well as their expertise on horseback. From veterans of the war a regiment was formed, and was accepted as the 3rd County of London (Sharpshooters), Imperial Yeomanry, in 1901.

During the Great War the 3rd CLY served in Egypt, Gallipoli, and in the campaigns in Palestine and Macedonia. It formed E Battalion, The Machine Gun Corps, in 1918 with the Rough Riders, being redesignated 103rd Battalion subsequently. The Battalion served in France from June 1918 to the end of the war.

The Regiment was reduced to an armoured car company in 1920 as part of the Tank Corps known as the 23rd (London) Armoured Car Company (Sharpshooters). Expanding in 1938 and converting to an armoured regiment, the Sharpshooters resumed their former title and formed a second regiment, the 4th County of London Yeomanry (Sharpshooters). Both regiments fought in the Western Desert, the 4th CLY particularly distinguishing itself at the Battle of El Alamein. Both regiments subsequently fought in Sicily and Italy. They landed in Normandy in June 1944, but suffering heavy casualties, were amalgamated in August 1944.

Remaining in tanks after the war, the 3/4th CLY was amalgamated in 1961 with the Kent Yeomanry, who had served as artillery since 1920 (qv).

King Edward's Horse (The King's Oversea Dominions Regiment)

The Regiment was raised in 1901 as 4th County of London Yeomanry (The King's Colonials). It originally comprised expatriates from the dominions and colonies, with squadrons affiliated to the Dominions by name. The title was changed to 'King Edward's Horse (The King's Oversea Dominions Regiment)' in 1910. In 1913 it was judged that Territorial Force terms of service were not entirely suitable for the regiment; accordingly it was transferred to the Special Reserve, thereby losing its Yeomanry status.

On mobilisation two regiments were formed almost immediately. From April 1915 to June 1916 individual squadrons of 1st KEH served in France as divisional cavalry. They were re-grouped as a corps cavalry regiment. The Regiment served in Italy from December 1917–March 1918. On return to France it was once more split up and squadrons served separately until the end of the war. 2nd KEH served in France from May 1915 to May 1916, not always as a complete unit. In June 1916 it was reinforced by a section of 21st Lancers and re-grouped as a corps cavalry regiment, and as such served until August 1917. The Regiment was then broken up and the personnel largely absorbed into the Tank Corps.

King Edward's Horse remained in the Army List until disbandment in 1924.

EAST LOTHIAN (HADDINGTON)

In 1797 three troops of Yeomanry were raised in East Lothian and renewed service in 1802.

In 1828 a corps was raised in Haddington and served without pay until 1831, but no troops existed from 1838 to 1846. The East Lothian Yeomanry was re-raised that year. In 1848 the Berwickshire Yeomanry Cavalry troop joined the East Lothian Yeomanry. In 1888 the Midlothian, and in 1892 the West Lothian

In this nostalgic picture, an NCO of a Yeomanry Armoured Car Company sees a vision of a cavalry charge during the Great War. The artist, Gilbert Holiday, is best known for his paintings of events depicting Royal Artillery horses and guns and hunting scenes.

– Royal Wiltshire Yeomanry

Corps joined the East Lothians, and the title the Lothians and Berwickshire Yeomanry was given to the Regiment.

The Lothians and Border Horse

The Regiment was redesignated The Lothians and Border Horse in 1908. For service in South Africa, it provided the 19th Company of the 6th Bn, Imperial Yeomanry. During the 1914–18 War the Regiment was divided, A and D Squadrons serving separately as divisional cavalry in France in 1915 and together forming the XII Corps Cavalry Regiment in Salonika from November of that year until the end of the war. 'RHQ' and 'B' Squadron served with the Glasgow Yeomanry as V Corps Cavalry Regiment and were later dismounted and absorbed into the 17th Bn, The Royal Scots.

After the war the 19th (Lothians & Border Horse) Armoured Car Company was formed, and in 1939 it was expanded into two regiments. The 1st moved to France as a tank regiment with the BEF and the survivors came out through Dunkirk. Re-formed, the Regiment landed in Normandy in 1944 and fought through to Holland and Germany. The 2nd Lothians and Border Horse landed in Algeria in December 1942 and fought in the Western Desert campaign. In March 1944 the Regiment moved to Italy and took part in the campaign, including fighting at the Battle of Cassino.

In 1947 the two Regiments re-formed as one in the armoured role, but in 1956 the Lothians and Border Horse joined the Lanarkshire and Glasgow Yeomanry Regiments to form the Queen's Own Lowland Yeomanry as an armoured regiment. After serving in the Royal Corps of Transport, the Lothians and Border Horse re-formed in 1992 as HQ Squadron of the Scottish Yeomanry.

WEST LOTHIAN (LINLITHGOW)

In 1803 a troop was raised in Linlithgow and served until 1827. Later, in the 1870s, a Yeomanry corps was again raised in the county, and in 1892 joined with the troops of the Lothians and Berwickshire Yeomanry Cavalry (qv).

MIDLOTHIAN

There had been volunteer cavalry in Edinburgh at various times (with which Sir Walter Scott was connected). The Royal Midlothian Yeomanry Cavalry was formed in 1800 but disbanded in 1828. It was affiliated to the Life Guards at the express wish of the Duke of Wellington. Yeomanry was again raised in the county in 1888 and amalgamated with the East Lothian Yeomanry (qv).

ISLE OF MAN

An unofficial body of mounted troops was formed in 1793 as the Manx Constitutional Dragoons, but the first Yeomanry corps was accepted in 1796 as the Manx Yeomanry Cavalry. They were used by the Excise and, on one occasion, when working with a press gang, 'apprehended some smugglers as proper persons to serve in the Navy'. They were often called upon by the Civil Authorities, but by 1825 only one troop was recorded as being in existence.

MONMOUTHSHIRE

The two troops of Yeomanry in Monmouthshire were closely associated with those in Gloucestershire. In 1798 the Chepstow Troop of Gentlemen and Yeomanry Cavalry and the Loyal Monmouthshire Troop were formed, the latter in the county town. They were accepted for service again in 1803 and continued at least until 1827.

MONTGOMERYSHIRE

The Montgomeryshire Yeomanry

The Montgomeryshire Corps was raised in 1803, but disbanded in 1828. Re-raised in 1831, it served without a break and at one time consisted of six troops. In the South African war it provided four companies, the 31st and 49th Companies for the 9th Bn, and the 88th and 89th Companies. For many years the Regiment was connected with the Williams Wynn family.

The Regiment served in England until March 1916 when it moved to Egypt to serve dismounted in the Western Frontier Force. It served in Palestine; forming the 25th (Montgomeryshire and Welsh Horse Yeomanry) Bn, Royal Welch Fusiliers, in 1917. In May 1918 the Battalion moved to France and remained there until the end of the war.

In 1920 the Montgomeryshire Yeomanry was absorbed into the Royal Welch Fusiliers as the 7th (Montgomeryshire) Battalion, and the Yeomanry title was never revived.

NORFOLK

The Norfolk Yeomanry (The King's Own Royal Regiment)

The Norfolk Rangers were raised by Colonel The Hon. George Townshend, later Marquis, and commissioned in 1782. They comprised a troop of cavalry and one

A sergeant with his three sons all serving in the Norfolk Yeomanry at the same time before the Great War. Such diminutive boy soldiers were often employed; these two are carrying bugles rather than cavalry trumpets.

– Suffolk and Norfolk Yeomanry

of foot soldiers. They were accepted as Yeomanry Cavalry in 1794. By 1828 there were three regiments; the 1st West, 2nd Mid and 3rd East Regiments of Yeomanry Cavalry. One regiment was re-raised in 1831, largely comprising members of the former Mid Regiment, but was disbanded in 1849. For a time there was a corps called the Norfolk and Suffolk Borderers. Light Horse Volunteers served in the County from 1862–7. A new regiment of Yeomanry was raised in 1901 at the express wish of the King; they were granted the 'Royal' suffix from the start.

The Norfolk Yeomanry landed for dismounted service in Gallipoli in October 1915, and on withdrawal to Egypt, manned Canal defences. In 1917 it was redesignated 12th (Norfolk Yeomanry) Bn. The Norfolk Regiment and took part, first in the Palestine campaign, and for the last few months of the war on the Western Front with the 31st Division.

The Norfolk Yeomanry was converted to artillery in 1920 and for a short time stood alone as a two-battery army field brigade. In 1923 the Brigade was redesignated 108 (Suffolk and Norfolk Yeomanry) Brigade, RFA and absorbed two Suffolk Yeomanry batteries (qv). In 1938 the Brigade was converted to the anti-tank role and redesignated 55th (Suffolk & Norfolk Yeomanry) Anti-Tank Regiment, RA. A 'duplicate' regiment was formed in 1939. In 1942 the batteries designated 'Norfolk Yeomanry' of each regiment were re-regimented as the 65th (Norfolk Yeomanry) Anti-Tank Regiment, RA. It served in France in 1940, then in the Western Desert, including the battle of Alamein, and subsequently in Italy before landing in Normandy on D-Day.

In 1947 the Norfolk Yeomanry reformed as 389th (Norfolk Yeomanry) Light Anti Aircraft Regiment, RA. Further amalgamations in the anti-aircraft role followed, then in 1961 the Regiment amalgamated again with the Suffolk Yeomanry as 308th (Suffolk and Norfolk) Field Regiment, RA. The present day successor is 202 (Suffolk & Norfolk Yeomanry), Field Battery, 100th (Yeomanry) Field Regiment, RA(V).

NORTHAMPTONSHIRE

The Northamptonshire Yeomanry

A regiment was formed in 1794 by Earl Spencer and was in existence until 1828. Two years later independent troops were raised, which served for a number of years, the last one, the Royal Kettering Troop, being disbanded in 1873.

In 1902 a new regiment was raised. It served in France from November 1914, the squadrons being divided between various formations. Reconstituted as VI Corps Cavalry Regiment in 1916, it later served in Italy before returning to France for the last month of the war.

In 1922 the Regiment was reduced in strength and became the 25th (Northamptonshire Yeomanry) Armoured Car Company, The Tank Corps (TA), the 'Royal' suffix being granted in 1923. Just prior to mobilisation the Company was expanded and formed into an armoured regiment, which was itself 'duplicated' and the regiments called the 1st and 2nd Northamptonshire Yeomanry. Both regiments landed in Normandy in June 1944. The 1st served across France, Belgium, Holland and into Germany, taking part in the amphibious crossing of the Rhine. The 2nd Regiment was disbanded in August 1944 and the members drafted to other regiments.

In 1947 the Regiment was re-formed as an armoured regiment, and it joined with the Inns of Court Regiment in 1961. Conversion to engineers took place in 1963, the title being 250 (Northamptonshire Yeomanry) Field Squadron, R.E., but this unit was disbanded in 1967.

NORTHUMBERLAND

The Northumberland Hussars

The Newcastle Troop was raised in 1797 but disbanded in 1802. In 1819 the Northumberland and Newcastle Regiment of Yeomanry Cavalry was raised and was retained in service under various titles to the present day. (Their nickname, 'The Noodles' has been in use for many years.)

The Regiment provided the 14th and 15th Companies of the 5th Bn, Imperial Yeomanry, for South Africa. During the 1914–18 War the Regiment reached Flanders in April 1915 and the squadrons were split up amongst various formations. In May 1916 it was re-formed as XIII Corps Cavalry Regiment and fought together for the remainder of the war. The 2/1st Northumberland Yeomanry served in England and Ireland until 1917 when it moved to France to fight as XIX Corps Cavalry Regiment. After five months it amalgamated with the 9th Battalion, The Northumberland Fusiliers, being redesignated the 9th (Northumberland Hussars Yeomanry) Battalion.

After the War, The Northumberland Hussars were reconstituted as a cavalry regiment but converted to artillery in 1940 as 102nd Light Anti-Aircraft/Anti-Tank Regiment, RA. On arrival in the Middle East the Anti-Aircraft battery left the Regiment. 102nd Anti-Tank Regiment served in Greece and Crete in 1941 and fought in the Western Desert with distinction, including at the Battle of El Alamein. It fought in Italy in 1943 and returned to England for the preparation for the Normandy invasion. Landing there on D-Day, the Regiment fought in north-west Europe for the rest of the war.

Re-formed in 1947 as a divisional regiment, RAC, the Northumberland Hussars were reduced temporarily to a cadre in 1968. At the present time D and HQ Squadrons of the Queen's Own Yeomanry are provided by the Northumberland Hussars.

NOTTINGHAMSHIRE

The Sherwood Rangers Yeomanry

Three troops were formed in 1794, and the Newark Troop survived the 1802 disbandments. In 1828 the Sherwood Rangers Yeomanry Cavalry was formed as a full regiment for service in that then turbulent county. To the present day the SRY has continued with unbroken service. It provided the 10th Company for the 3rd Bn, Imperial Yeomanry, for the South African war.

The Regiment moved to Egypt and in August 1915 sailed to Gallipoli with the 2nd Mounted Division for service as infantry. The Regiment returned to Egypt and, after service in Salonika, took part in the Palestine campaign.

Restored as cavalry in 1920 the Regiment retained its horses until 1940 when serving in the Middle East. After being equipped as lorried infantry, the Regiment became coastal gunners and served at the siege of Tobruk and the invasion of Crete. It was converted to an armoured regiment in 1941 and took part in the Desert Campaign, including fighting at Alam El Halfa and El Alamein. The Sherwood Rangers returned to England in December 1943, landed in Normandy on D-Day, and fought through north-west Europe until the end of the war.

The Regiment was reconstituted in 1947 as an armoured regiment. A successor squadron formed part of the Royal Yeomanry, but as B (Sherwood Rangers Yeomanry) Squadron now serves with the Queen's Own Yeomanry. A (Sherwood Rangers Yeomanry) Squadron, as infantry, formed part of the 3rd (Volunteer) Bn, The Worcestershire and Sherwood Foresters Regiment (29th/45th Foot) for some years.

This military period piece of 1902 depicts officers of the Sherwood Rangers Yeomanry practising observation, a lesson a fortiori *of the South African War.*

– Sherwood Rangers Yeomanry

The South Nottinghamshire Hussars

The Nottingham Troop was formed in 1794 but was disbanded in 1802. The Holme Pierrepont Troop was raised in 1798 and in 1826 was regimented as the South Nottinghamshire Regiment of Yeomanry Cavalry. Like its sister Regiment, the South Notts Hussars has been retained in continuous service until the present day. It formed the 12th Company of the 3rd Bn Imperial Yeomanry for the war in South Africa.

Brigaded with the Sherwood Rangers during the Great War, the Regiment was first sent to Egypt and then moved to Gallipoli to fight as infantry. The Regiment remained in the Middle East, serving in the Egyptian and Palestine campaigns, and in 1918 moved to the Western Front for conversion as the 100th Bn, The Machine Gun Corps with the Warwickshire Yeomanry.

In 1920 the Regiment converted to artillery and became 107th (South Notts Hussars Yeomanry) Brigade, RFA. As 107th Field Regiment it became RHA in 1938 and a 'duplicate' regiment, 150th Field Regiment, was formed in 1939. 107th Field Regiment served in Palestine and then at Tobruk, where, at the Battle of Knightsbridge, it sustained overwhelming casualties. Members who escaped re-formed into a Medium Battery and took part in the Battle of El Alamein. It then fought at the assault landings on Sicily before being re-constituted as a full regiment. Landing in July 1944 in Normandy, the Regiment fought to the end of the War in north-west Europe. 150th Regiment served first in the United Kingdom and landed in Normandy on D plus 2 and was in support of 6th Airborne Division. It served until November 1944 and was then disbanded.

In 1947 the two regiments were re-formed as 307th (South Notts Hussars Yeomanry) Field Regiment and 350th (South Notts Hussars Yeomanry) Heavy Regiment, RA. The RHA title was restored subsequently. The successor unit is 307 (South Notts Hussars Yeomanry RHA) Battery, RA(V) and the Band.

The South Notts Hussars on the march in Full Dress 1904.

– South Notts Hussars

This group of officers of the Queen's Own Oxfordshire Hussars, taken at Blenheim Palace c1905, gives a clear picture of their splendid full dress uniforms, the facings of which were 'Mantua purple'. The seated officers are Lord Valentia, the Duke of Marlborough, Winston Churchill and an unknown officer. After the Great War, Churchill was involved in the re-organisation of the Territorial Force.

– Royal Green Jackets Museum, Oxford

OXFORDSHIRE

The Queen's Own Oxfordshire Hussars

The North Wootton Troop was commissioned in 1798 and was regimented in 1818 to form the North-West Regiment of Oxfordshire Yeomanry Cavalry, later the 1st Regiment. There were many troops at different times in the county. The Oxfordshire Regiment of Yeomanry Cavalry was accepted in 1828 for service without pay but fully restored in 1830. The Regiment provided the 40th Company of the 10th Bn, Imperial Yeomanry, for the South African war.

On mobilisation in 1914, the Regiment went with the British Expeditionary Force to France. It remained mounted and served in a number of different formations in France and Flanders during the war.

The Oxfordshire Yeomanry was converted to artillery in 1920 and provided two batteries, 399 and 400 (QOOHY) Batteries in 100th (Worcestershire and Oxfordshire Yeomanry) Brigade, RFA. In 1938 the unit was converted to the anti-tank role as 53rd Anti-Tank Regiment. On 'duplication' in 1939 the Oxfordshire Yeomanry title was carried only by the 'duplicate' unit, 63rd Anti-Tank Regiment, which served in Home Forces until June 1944, then throughout the campaign in north-west Europe.

63rd Anti-Tank Regiment was re-formed in the post-war TA as 387th (Oxfordshire Yeomanry) Field Regiment. In 1950 387th Field Regiment was amalgamated with the Bucks Yeomanry as 299th (Royal Bucks Yeomanry and Queen's Own Oxfordshire Hussars) Field Regiment (see under Bucks Yeomanry). A successor sub-unit serves as 5 (Queen's Own Oxfordshire Hussars) Signal Squadron (V).

PEEBLESSHIRE

The Peeblesshire Yeomanry Cavalry

Sir James Montgomery, Bt, raised a troop of cavalry when war broke out afresh in 1803. It quickly reached a strength of 56 all ranks. In 1820, after the Radical disturbances, a second troop was raised, based in the village of Eddleston. The Peeblesshire Yeomanry Cavalry was reviewed on Portobello Sands by George IV in August 1822 with a number of other corps. It was disbanded in 1827.

PEMBROKESHIRE

The Pembroke (Castlemartin) Yeomanry

The Castlemartin Yeomanry was raised in 1794 and, despite serving without pay from 1828–31, the Regiment remained in being throughout the period. In 1842–3 the Castlemartin Yeomanry was on permanent duty for six months in aid of the Civil Power. The only Battle Honour won in Britain – 'Fishguard' – was awarded (in 1853) for the action against the French in 1797. The Pembroke Yeomanry provided the 30th Company of the 9th Bn, Imperial Yeomanry, for the South African war.

The Regiment served in England until 1916 when it moved to Egypt for dismounted service. It served in the Palestine campaign and became, in 1917, the 24th (Pembroke and Glamorgan Yeomanry) Bn, The Welch Regiment. The Battalion served in France for the last six months of the war.

In 1920 the Pembroke Yeomanry was re-constituted as artillery, forming 102nd (Pembroke and Cardigan) Brigade, RFA, and in 1938, 102nd Field Regiment, RA. This regiment landed in Algiers in February 1943 and became a medium regiment serving in the Italian campaign. 146 Field Regiment, RA, was formed from the Cardigan Battery in 1939 and served in the North African campaign from 1942, including fighting at El Alamein. Later the Regiment moved to north-west Europe after conversion to medium artillery.

In 1947 the Pembroke Yeomanry re-formed as 302 Field Regiment, RA, but from 1961 provided a squadron in the armoured reconnaissance role with the Shropshire Yeomanry. The successor unit is 224 (Pembrokeshire Yeomanry) Transport Squadron, Royal Logistic Corps (V).

PERTHSHIRE

The Scottish Horse

The Perthshire Yeomanry Cavalry was raised in June 1798 and served until 1808. It was raised again in 1817 and constituted independent troops until disbandment in 1828.

Lord Tullibardine, who later became the Duke of Atholl, accepted the offer of command of a regiment raised from Scotsmen living in South Africa. By February 1901 the Scottish Horse was four squadrons strong. A second regiment was raised shortly after from volunteers from Scotland and Australia and both regiments fought with distinction throughout the war.

Returning to Scotland, Lord Tullibardine raised two new regiments of Scottish Horse who were constituted as Yeomanry, the 1st Regiment recruiting from the county of Perthshire and the 2nd Regiment from Aberdeenshire, Elgin, Nairn

Some thirty years after raising the regiment, the Duke of Atholl addresses a younger generation of the Scottish Horse at Blair Atholl during annual camp

– Scottish Horse Museum

and Argyllshire. On the outbreak of war a third regiment and supporting units were authorised and the Scottish Horse became a Brigade under Brigadier Lord Tullibardine. The Scottish Horse fought dismounted in Gallipoli, Egypt, and the Scottish Horse Battalion (nominally the 13th Bn, The Black Watch) fought in Salonika and in 1918 on the Western Front. The 1/3 Scottish Horse provided 26 Squadron, the Machine Gun Corps, and continued to serve in Egypt.

The Scottish Horse retained a horsed role as 'scouts' until December 1939 when they converted to artillery, forming the 79th and 80th Medium Regiments, RA. The latter regiment moved to Egypt in 1943 and joining the Highland Division, fought in Sicily and through Italy including at the battle of Sangro. The 79th landed on Juno beach on 7 June 1944 and remained in action throughout the advance into Germany.

After the war the Scottish Horse re-formed as a divisional regiment, RAC, and formed part of the Highland Division. In 1956 the Regiment was amalgamated with the Fife and Forfar Yeomanry and later became known as the Highland Yeomanry in 1969. It is now represented in the Scottish Yeomanry.

RENFREWSHIRE

There appears to have been a corps of Yeomanry in Renfrewshire from 1795 until 1802. In 1813 four troops are recorded and service can be traced until 1839.

ROXBURGHSHIRE

The Roxburghshire Yeomanry Light Dragoons

The Western and Eastern Troops of the Roxburghshire Gentlemen and Yeomanry Cavalry were raised in 1797 and commanded by Sir James Pringle, Bt, of Stichell. The Jedburgh troop was called out in August, only three months after formation, to quell rioting. The Corps became known as the Roxburghshire Yeomanry Light

Dragoons with an establishment of three troops, later increased to four in 1820 and five in 1821. The Corps was on parade for the Royal Visit to Edinburgh in 1822 when detachments of Berwickshire, Peebleshire, East Lothian, Royal Midlothian, West Lothian, Selkirkshire Light Dragoons, Royal Fifeshire, Stirlingshire and Clackmannan and Kinross corps also paraded. The Regiment was disbanded in 1828.

In 1872 the 1st Roxburghshire (The Border) Mounted Rifle Volunteer Corps was formed, but was disbanded twenty years later.

RUTLAND

It is believed that the first Yeomanry corps to be accepted under the Act of 1794 was raised in Rutland by the Earl of Winchilsea in April 1794. It was called the Rutland Light Dragoons, comprising three troops. Later they appear to have been absorbed into the Rutland Legion which disappeared in 1825. Closely associated with the Leicestershire Regiment of Yeomanry Cavalry from the beginning, men from Rutland served in that Regiment from early in the nineteenth century.

SELKIRKSHIRE

The Selkirkshire Yeomanry Light Dragoons

The Selkirkshire Corps of Yeomanry Cavalry was formed in January 1798 and, after confirming their willingness to serve after the Peace of Amiens, became known as the Selkirkshire Yeomanry Light Dragoons. At the time of the 'False Alarm' in 1804 some members of the Troop rode 70 miles within the day to muster at Dalkeith. Only one troop was formed, and with so many other corps, disbandment occurred in 1828. An attempt in 1859 to form the 'Volunteer Ettrick Forest Carabineers' or 'Ettrick Forest Mounted Rifles' came to naught.

SHROPSHIRE

The Shropshire Yeomanry

Two troops of Yeomanry were formed in 1795 at Wellington and Market Drayton. In early years there were eleven corps in the county, including the Wrekin Company, Hales Owen Cavalry, Pimhill Light Horse and Oswestry Rangers. The Brimstree Loyal Legion had served for some years but disbanded in 1802. In 1814 the existing corps were regimented, forming respectively the South Shropshire, Shrewsbury, and North Shropshire Yeomanry Cavalry regiments. The first two amalgamated in 1828 to form the South Salopian Yeomanry Cavalry, and the North Shropshire regiment changed its name to North Salopian Yeomanry Cavalry. The two regiments then amalgamated in 1872. Volunteers from the Shropshire Yeomanry formed the 13th Company of the 5th Bn, Imperial Yeomanry for the South African war.

During the First World War the Shropshire Yeomanry served dismounted in Egypt from March 1916, initially as part of 4 Dismounted Brigade. A year later it was amalgamated with the Cheshire Yeomanry to form the 10th (Shropshire and Cheshire Yeomanry) Bn, The King's Shropshire Light Infantry as part of the 74th

(Yeomanry) Division. The Battalion fought in the Palestine campaign and in France and Belgium from May 1918 until the end of the war.

In 1920 the mounted role was restored to the Regiment, but in 1940 conversion to artillery took place. As the 75th and 76th Medium Regiment, RA they both fought in the Middle East and Italy.

In 1947 the Regiment converted to armour and became a divisional regiment RAC. It later was re-equipped with armoured cars. Incorporating the Pembrokeshire Yeomanry and Shropshire RHA (1967), the Regiment was subsequently reduced in 1969 to a cadre and a signal squadron, later the 95 (Shropshire Yeomanry) Signal Squadron (V). In 1971 a squadron was formed from the cadre for the Queen's Own Mercian Yeomanry subsequently Royal Mercian and Lancastrian Yeomanry. This now has a home defence reconnaissance role.

SOMERSET

The North Somerset Yeomanry

The Frome Troop was accepted for service in 1798 but with later-formed troops – the Bath, Wells, Rode and Wolverton, and Beckington troops – was disbanded in 1802. The Frome Troop was re-raised a year later and, in 1804, formed, with the East Mendip Corps, the Frome and East Mendip Regiment of Yeomanry Cavalry. In 1814 it was renamed the North Somerset Yeomanry. It formed the 48th Company of the 7th Bn, Imperial Yeomanry for the South African war.

In November 1914 the North Somerset Yeomanry moved to France and served in various formations on the Western Front. It was withdrawn from the Front in 1918 but re-formed as a mounted regiment and subsequently it sent individual squadrons to regular cavalry regiments for the remainder of the war.

The North Somerset Yeomanry resumed the mounted role and at the start of the Second World War served in the Middle East. In 1942 the Regiment converted to a signal role as 4th Air Formation Signals, the task being to provide communications between the Army and the RAF. Subsequently the Regiment moved to Sicily and Italy. In 1944 it was redesignated 14th Air Formation Signals and served in the campaign in north-west Europe.

In 1947 the North Somerset Yeomanry re-formed as an airportable Divisional Regiment, RAC. In 1956 it amalgamated with the 44th Royal Tank Regiment and in 1965 was redesignated the North Somerset and Bristol Yeomanry. In 1967 the Regiment was absorbed into the infantry and the successors serve in the 6th Bn, The Light Infantry (V).

The West Somerset Yeomanry

The Bridgwater Troop of the West Somerset Yeomanry Cavalry dates from 1794, and the regiment from 1798. It served without pay from 1828–31 and did not disband. (Inaccuracies in tracing its history when the order of precedence was being argued, led to loss of precedence; it had allegedly maintained continuous service since 1794.) West Somerset yeomen served in the 48th Company of the 7th Bn, Imperial Yeomanry, in the South African war.

The West Somerset Yeomanry was sent to Gallipoli in October 1915. It moved to Egypt, served as infantry, and fought with the Western Frontier Force. It was redesignated 12th (West Somerset Yeomanry) Bn, The Somerset Light Infantry in January 1917, and joined the 74th (Yeomanry) Division on its formation in March. The Battalion served in the Palestine campaign and in France from May 1918.

The West Somerset Yeomanry was amalgamated in 1920 with the Dorset Yeomanry and the Somerset Royal Horse Artillery to form 94th (Dorset and Somerset Yeomanry) Brigade, RFA, in which two batteries, 373 and 374, were designated 'West Somerset Yeomanry'. The amalgamation was short-lived, however, and the two West Somerset Yeomanry batteries were transferred to 55 (Wessex) Field Brigade, RA. A 'duplicate' unit, 112th Field Regiment, RA, was formed in 1939. 55th Field Regiment served in Home Forces, joining the Guards Armoured Division in 1941 and fighting with the Division throughout the campaign in north-west Europe. 112nd Field Regiment also served in north-west Europe.

The original unit was re-formed as 255th (Wessex) Medium Regiment, RA, in 1947, later redesignated 'West Somerset Yeomanry'. In 1961 the Regiment amalgamated once more with the Dorset Yeomanry (qv) to form 250th (Queen's Own Dorset and West Somerset Yeomanry) Medium Regiment. It was later absorbed into the infantry in 1967.

The East Somerset Yeomanry Cavalry

The Castle Cary Troop was raised in 1794 and later the East Somerset Regiment of Yeomanry Cavalry was formed. Serving through the period of peace in 1802–3, it was disbanded in 1828, except for the Taunton Troop which continued until 1843. A separate troop, the Ilminster Troop, served from 1831–47.

STAFFORDSHIRE

The Staffordshire Yeomanry (Queen's Own Royal Regiment)

The Regiment of Staffordshire Yeomanry Cavalry was commissioned in 1794 and has served without disbandment to the present day. In 1808 twelve troops of this Regiment are recorded, and during its early years it was probably called out in aid of the Civil Power more times than any other regiment. The Royal title was conferred in 1838. Two companies were formed for the South African War, the 6th Company and the 106th Company, both for the 4th Bn, Imperial Yeomanry.

The Regiment formed part of 22 Mounted Brigade in the Great War and fought in the Egyptian and Palestine campaigns from 1915, taking part in the capture of Damascus in 1918.

The Staffordshire Yeomanry retained its horses until 1941 when it converted to armour and fought in the Western Desert including the Battle of El Alamein. It then returned to England. The Regiment landed on D Day and fought throughout the campaign in north-west Europe.

In 1947 it was re-formed as an armoured regiment and, in 1958, as an armoured car regiment. In 1969 the Staffordshire Yeomanry cadre of three officers and five other ranks was attached to 23 SAS Regiment. In 1971 it was expanded to a squadron, and, as B (Queen's Own Royal Staffordshire Yeomanry) Squadron, joined The Queen's Own Mercian Yeomanry.

Lieutenant-Colonel William Murray of Polmaise, Vice Lieutenant of Stirlingshire and in Command of the Stirlingshire Yeomanry Cavalry for many years, in the uniform of the Regiment. Painted in 1828 by Sir Watson Gordon.

– In a private collection

STIRLINGSHIRE

The Stirlingshire Yeomanry Cavalry

In 1798 the Stirlingshire Yeomanry Cavalry was formed by William Murray of Polmaise, and by 1803 it comprised six troops. At the time of the insurrection in Scotland in 1820 four troops were called out – Stirling, Falkirk, Kilsyth and Fintry Troops. (For some unexplained reason the Campsie Troop was not called out.) The Regiment was still serving in the 1830s.

SUFFOLK

The Duke of York's Own Loyal Suffolk Hussars

A number of troops, raised in Suffolk in 1793, were accepted in 1794 as Yeomanry Cavalry. Six troops were regimented in 1814 to form the 1st Regiment of Loyal Suffolk Yeomanry Cavalry. Disbanded in 1827, they were accepted for service in 1831, and, in 1868, the 1st Loyal Suffolk Yeomanry amalgamated with the Long Melford troop to form the West Suffolk Regiment of Yeomanry Cavalry. The Eye troop was known as the Suffolk and Norfolk Borderers, which is also recorded with the order of the counties reversed. The Regiment's title was changed to the Loyal Suffolk Hussars in 1875 and the Duke of York (later King George V) became Honorary Colonel in 1894. Two companies of the 12th Bn, Imperial Yeomanry, were provided for the South African war, the 43rd and 44th Companies.

The Regiment served for two months in 1915 in Gallipoli. On withdrawal to Egypt it served dismounted on Canal defences, becoming in 1917 the 15th Bn, The Suffolk Regiment. The Battalion served in Palestine and moved to France in May 1918 as part of the 74th (Yeomanry) Division.

The Suffolk Yeomanry was converted to artillery in 1920 and initially provided two batteries, 411 and 412 (Suffolk Yeomanry) Batteries in 103 Brigade, RFA. The two batteries were shortly transferred to 108 Brigade, RFA, which was redesignated 'Suffolk and Norfolk Yeomanry'. In 1938 the Brigade was converted to the anti-tank role as 55th (Suffolk & Norfolk Yeomanry) Anti-Tank Regiment, RA. A 'duplicate' unit, 65th Anti-Tank Regiment, was formed in 1939. In 1942 all four Suffolk Yeomanry batteries were regimented as 55th Anti-Tank Regiment which was designated 'Suffolk Yeomanry'. The Regiment served in Home Forces until landing on the Normandy Beaches on D plus 6. It continued to fight in north-west Europe until the end of the War.

The Suffolk Yeomanry was reformed in 1947 as 308th (Suffolk Yeo) Anti-Tank Regiment, RA. Further amalgamations took place, all with the 'Suffolk Yeomanry' title as 308 Field Regiment, RA. The successor unit is 202 (Suffolk and Norfolk Yeo) Field Battery in 100th (Yeomanry) Field Regiment, RA(V).

The Duke of York (later King George V) watches his regiment of Loyal Suffolk Hussars march past during a parade in 1893 at Ickworth Park, Bury St Edmunds.
– Suffolk & Norfolk Yeomanry

A patrol of the Surrey Yeomanry (Queen Mary's Regiment) Gloucester Post, Salonika. After a watercolour painting by F. A. Stewart, an officer of the Regiment.

– Colonel A. Constance/ Surrey Yeomanry

SURREY

The Surrey Yeomanry (Queen Mary's Regiment)

The Surrey Gentlemen and Yeomanry Cavalry was raised in 1794, with six troops formed into a regiment, and twelve independent troops. They were disbanded in 1828. The Southwark Troop, raised in 1831, became a full regiment in the same year. It was disbanded in 1848. The Surrey Imperial Yeomanry was raised in 1901 and was granted the Princess of Wales's title, later to be altered to 'Queen Mary's' on the accession of George V.

In late 1914 the Regiment was divided in support of various formations. B and C Squadrons served mounted in Egypt in 1915, the latter moving to France in 1916 to form part of a corps cavalry regiment and being eventually absorbed in the 10th Bn, Royal West Surrey Regiment. A Squadron moved to Salonika in 1916 and was joined by B Squadron in the XVI Corps Cavalry Regiment. It remained in Macedonia until 1918.

In 1922 the Surrey Yeomanry was re-formed with two batteries of guns, as part of the 98th (Surrey and Sussex Yeomanry) Brigade, RFA, the batteries being designated with individual county titles. (For their history see under Sussex Yeomanry.)

In 1947 the Surrey Yeomanry was re-formed as a separate regiment, 298th (Surrey Yeomanry, Queen Mary's) Field Regiment, RA. It later amalgamated with 263rd Field Regiment which served until 1967. The successor units are A Company 6/7 Bn Princess of Wales's Royal Regiment and 127 (Surrey and Sussex) Field Squadron RE(V).

SUSSEX

The Sussex Yeomanry

Various troops of Yeomanry Cavalry were accepted for service in 1794 but they were disbanded in 1828. (Some troops were of different composition and role, viz. Guides, a Legion, and Yeomanry Horse Artillery.) The Petworth, Arundel and Bramber corps were raised in 1831 but had all disbanded by August 1848. A Brighton Troop was serving with the Middlesex Hussars in the 1880s. In 1901 a new regiment, The Sussex Imperial Yeomanry, was formed, the 69th Company Imperial Yeomanry having been raised in 1900 in the county for service in South Africa.

The Regiment served at Gallipoli in late 1915 and then withdrew to Egypt. It served mainly in the dismounted role on Canal defences and then formed the 16th Bn (Sussex Yeomanry), The Royal Sussex Regiment. It fought in the Palestine campaign and in 1917 moved to France where it served until the end of the war.

In 1922 the Sussex Yeomanry was amalgamated with the Surrey Yeomanry after conversion to artillery, as 98th (Surrey and Sussex Yeomanry) Brigade, RFA, in which two batteries, 389 and 390, were designated 'Sussex Yeomanry'. A 'duplicate' unit, the 144th Field Regiment, RA, was raised in 1939 and it was into this regiment that the two Sussex Yeomanry batteries were concentrated, the Surrey Yeomanry batteries forming the nucleus of the 98th Field Regiment.

For the first year of the war 144th Field Regiment served in the United Kingdom until, at the end of 1940, it was sent to the Sudan, whence it moved to Egypt, Libya, Iraq, Persia and Palestine. 98th Field Regiment fought in France with the British Expeditionary Force before Dunkirk and, after re-forming, went to North Africa. It took part in the Battle of El Alamein with 10th Armoured Division. It subsequently fought with SP guns in the Italian campaign, and saw action at the fighting for Monte Cassino.

In 1947 the Sussex Yeomanry re-formed as 344th Light Anti-Aircraft and Searchlight Regiment, RA, later amalgamating to form, at first, 258th LAA Regiment and, in 1961, 257th Field Regiment. The successor unit served as 200 (Sussex Yeomanry) Field Battery RA(V) for some years, but is now 127 (Surrey and Sussex Yeomanry) Field Squadron RE, in 78 Fortress Engineer Regiment (V).

WALES

The Welsh Horse

The Welsh Horse was raised as a Yeomanry Regiment in August 1914 in South Wales. In September 1915 it landed in Gallipoli and fought dismounted. On the withdrawal to Egypt at the end of that year, it manned the Canal defences. It amalgamated in 1916 and formed the 25th (Montgomeryshire and Welsh Horse Yeomanry) Bn, The Royal Welch Fusiliers, and fought in the Palestine campaign, moving to France for the last six months of the war. It was disbanded in 1919.

Although it was the last Yeomanry regiment to be raised, it was accorded seniority after the Glamorgan Yeomanry because of its connexion with the Glamorgan TA Association at the time of formation in 1914.

WARWICKSHIRE

The Warwickshire Yeomanry

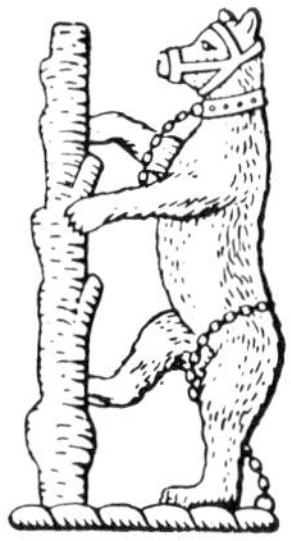

The Warwickshire Yeomanry is second in order of seniority of all the Yeomanry regiments, troops having been raised in July 1794. It became a regiment in 1797 and due to its frequent involvement in providing aid to the Civil Power, it was never disbanded. For the South African war the Regiment provided the 5th Company of the 2nd Bn, Imperial Yeomanry and was constantly engaged with the enemy.

In August 1915 the Warwickshire Yeomanry was sent from Egypt to fight dismounted at Gallipoli and remained there for three months before withdrawal. Reforming in Egypt, the regiment remained a mounted cavalry regiment as part of the Desert Mounted Corps and fought throughout the Palestine campaign, taking part at the famous charge at Huj with the Worcestershire Yeomanry. In the final months of the war, the Warwickshire Yeomanry moved to Italy and France and, joining with the South Notts Hussars, formed the 100th Bn, The Machine Gun Corps.

'The smartest section in the Brigade'. This photograph shows Yeomen of the Warwickshire Yeomanry during the Palestine Campaign when they were part of the 5th Mounted Brigade.

– Worcester City Museum and Art Gallery/ Worcestershire Yeomanry

Returning to Palestine in 1939 as a cavalry regiment, the Warwickshire Yeomanry was converted to lorried infantry and finally to a tank regiment as part of 9 Armoured Brigade. It fought at El Alamein and later throughout the Campaigns in Italy.

In 1947 the Regiment was re-formed as an armoured regiment and in 1956 amalgamated with the Worcestershire Yeomanry. Reduced to a cadre in 1969, it was expanded again in 1971. The two successor squadrons are A (Queen's Own Warwickshire and Worcestershire Yeomanry) Squadron of the Royal Mercian and Lancastrian Yeomanry, and 67 (Queen's Own Warwickshire and Worcestershire Yeomanry) Signal Squadron (V) which is part of 37th (Worcestershire & Welsh) Signal Regiment (V).

WESTMORLAND

The Westmorland and Cumberland Yeomanry

The Westmorland Yeomanry Cavalry was raised in October 1819 comprising six troops (two of which were found from Cumberland). The Regiment remained in

The Earl of Lonsdale inspects his Regiment the Westmorland and Cumberland Yeomanry. A very great sportsman, he also threw his enormous energy into military affairs, often to the despair of the authorities. The Regiment, which he treated almost as if it were his private army, formed a guard of Honour for the Kaiser during his visit to Lowther Castle in 1895.

– R. Hasell McCosh Esq

being in 1828, but served without pay until 1831. In 1843 it became known as the Westmorland and Cumberland Yeomanry Cavalry, and for a hundred years the two families of Lowther and Hasell were intimately connected with it. The Regiment provided the 24th Company of the 8th Bn, Imperial Yeomanry.

On mobilisation the Regiment remained in England and then divided the squadrons amongst three infantry divisions. Joining together again in 1917, the Regiment was the XI Corps Cavalry Regiment and fought dismounted from 1917 with 7th (Westmorland and Cumberland Yeomanry) Battalion, The Border Regiment.

The Westmorland and Cumberland Yeomanry was converted to artillery in 1920 and formed a two-battery army field brigade, 93rd (Westmorland and Cumberland Yeo) Brigade, RFA, in which 369 and 370 Batteries were designated respectively 'Westmorland Yeomanry' and 'Cumberland Yeomanry'. These two batteries were shortly transferred to 51st (Westmorland and Cumberland) Field Brigade which had two other non-Yeomanry batteries. On 'duplication' in 1939, 369 Battery went into the 'duplicate' unit, 109th Field Regiment, while 370 Battery stayed with the original Regiment. 370 Battery was in action in Norway in 1940, and 51st Field Regiment fought at Tobruk in 1941 and with the Chindit Brigade in Burma. 109th Field Regiment remained for home defence for the duration of the war.

Both regiments were re-formed in 1947, as 251st and 309th (Westmorland and Cumberland) Field Regiments, RA. They were amalgamated, as 251st Field Regiment, in 1950 and later redesignated as 'Westmorland and Cumberland Yeomanry'. In 1961 the Regiment was reduced to an independent battery as 851 (Westmorland and Cumberland Yeomanry) Field Battery, RA and briefly served as TAVR III infantry before disbandment.

WIGTOWNSHIRE

A troop was formed in Wigtown in 1797 and appears to have remained in service until the 1820s. In 1811 the Galloway Rangers Corps was formed and served for some years. Two troops were re-raised in 1831, one in Wigtown and the other in Stranraer.

WILTSHIRE

The Royal Wiltshire Yeomanry (Prince of Wales's Own)

Ten troops of Yeomanry were commissioned in 1794, and were regimented in 1797 as the Regiment of Wiltshire Yeomanry Cavalry. It has served ever since and accorded seniority as the first regiment in the order of precedence. It was given the prefix 'Royal' in 1831 and 'Prince of Wales's Own' in 1863. The practice of incorporating 'dismounted' riflemen was begun in 1859 but discontinued in 1876. Two companies were provided for the South African war the 1st and 2nd Companies of the 1st Bn, Imperial Yeomanry. A third company was drafted abroad later.

In 1915 the Regiment was divided and joined various corps cavalry regiments in France. In 1916 the squadrons formed the XV Corps Cavalry Regiment but a year later it was dismounted and became the 6th (Wiltshire Yeomanry) Bn, The Wiltshire Regiment. It was later absorbed into other battalions, including the 9th Dorsets.

The Royal Wiltshire Yeomanry retained its cavalry role between the wars and went to the Middle East as a mounted cavalry regiment in 1940. It then served as lorried infantry in the Iraq, Syrian and Persian campaigns: one squadron served as searchlight troops at Tobruk. The Regiment was converted to armour in time to feature in the initial breakthrough at the battle of El Alamein as part of 9 Armoured Brigade supporting the New Zealand Division. Suffering heavy losses, the Regiment was withdrawn, subsequently taking part in the Italian campaign.

In 1947 the Royal Wiltshire Yeomanry re-formed as a divisional regiment, RAC, and later adopted the reconnaissance role. It was reduced in 1967 to one squadron, but the second was restored in 1971. The two remaining squadrons of the Royal Wiltshire Yeomanry serve as A Squadron of the Royal Yeomanry and B Squadron of the Royal Wessex Yeomanry, both in the reconnaissance role.

WORCESTERSHIRE

The Queen's Own Worcestershire Hussars

The Worcestershire Yeomanry was raised in 1794 by the Hon J. Somers-Cocks (later Earl Somers). It was disbanded in 1827 but re-raised in 1831.

The Regiment provided the 16th Company of the 5th Bn, Imperial Yeomanry, during the Boer War. During the Great War the Worcestershire Yeomanry went first to Egypt as part of the 2nd Mounted Division, and then served in Gallipoli from August 1915. Returning to Egypt the Regiment subsequently fought in the Palestine Campaign after being reconstituted following the bloody battle at Quatia. It took part in the charge at Huj and the capture of the Turkish guns.

In 1920 the Worcestershire Yeomanry was converted to artillery and provided two batteries, 397 and 398 in 100th (Worcestershire and Oxfordshire Yeomanry) Brigade, RFA. Both batteries were designated 'Queen's Own Worcestershire Hussars Yeomanry'. The unit was re-roled as an anti-tank regiment in 1938 and designated 53rd Anti-Tank Regiment, the two Worcestershire Yeomanry batteries becoming 209 and 210 Anti-Tank Batteries. A 'duplicate' unit, 63rd Anti-Tank Regiment was raised in 1939 and the Worcestershire Yeomanry batteries were concentrated in the original unit. 53rd Anti-Tank Regiment served with the BEF in 1940 and then joined 6th Airborne Division as 53rd Airlanding

Light Regiment. As such it took part in the airborne invasion of Normandy and in the measures to counter the Ardennes offensive.

The Regiment was reformed as 300th (Worcestershire Yeomanry) Anti-Tank Regiment, RA in 1947 but in 1950 was transferred to the Royal Armoured Corps as The Queen's Own Worcestershire Hussars. It served as such until amalgamation with the Warwickshire Yeomanry in 1956' (qv).

YORKSHIRE (WEST RIDING)

The Yorkshire Hussars (Alexandra, Princess of Wales's Own)

Formed in August 1794 as the 2nd or Northern Regiment of West Riding Yeomanry Cavalry and in 1802 becoming the 1st Regiment, it was never disbanded. In this year it numbered eight troops and adopted the name Hussars in the 1820s. For the South African war it provided the 9th Company of the 3rd Battalion and part of the 66th Company, Imperial Yeomanry.

In 1915 the Regiment was divided between various divisions for service in France and in May 1916 re-formed as XVII Corps Cavalry Regiment. In 1917 it was dismounted and became the 9th (Yorkshire Hussars Yeomanry) Bn, the West Yorkshire Regiment, continuing to serve on the Western Front until the ending of the war.

The Yorkshire Hussars were re-formed as a cavalry regiment after the war. From 1940–2 it served in the 5th and 6th Cavalry Brigades in Palestine. Converting to an armoured regiment, the Yorkshire Hussars remained in the Middle East until 1943, when it returned to the United Kingdom.

After the Second World War the Regiment became an armoured regiment. In 1956 it was reduced to a squadron as part of The Queen's Own Yorkshire Yeomanry. After further reduction to a cadre in 1969, the Yorkshire Squadron of the Queen's Own Yeomanry was formed in 1971 as a sabre squadron.

The Yorkshire Dragoons (The Queen's Own)

The 1st or Southern Regiment of West Riding Yeomanry Cavalry was raised in August 1794 but disbanded in 1802 and lost precedence thereby. A year later it was re-raised and became the 2nd or Southern Regiment. Further changes in name occurred when it became the South West Yorkshire Cavalry, and later the 1st West Yorkshire Yeomanry Cavalry. In 1897 the title was changed to the Queen's Own Yorkshire Yeomanry Dragoons.

The Regiment provided the 11th Company of the 3rd Bn, Imperial Yeomanry and, with the Yorkshire Hussars, provided the 66th Company, the two West Riding Regiments together providing 1,700 men for South Africa.

In 1915 the Yorkshire Dragoons were divided between various corps cavalry regiments in France, but in 1916 re-formed as II Corps Cavalry Regiment. In early 1918, it was dismounted and became a cyclist battalion for the rest of the war.

The Yorkshire Dragoons retained their cavalry role after the Great War and, as part of the 5th Cavalry Brigade, served from 1940–2 in Palestine and Syria. They were the last horsed regiment on active service in the British Army. Converting to a motor battalion, the Regiment fought at El Alamein. They were redesignated 9th Bn, KOYLI in late 1942 and as such served in the Italian campaign.

Re-formed as an armoured regiment in 1947, the Yorkshire Dragoons were amalgamated with the other two regiments to form The Queen's Own Yorkshire Yeomanry in 1956 (qv under Yorkshire Hussars).

The Prince of Wales's Own 2nd West Yorkshire Yeomanry Cavalry

This Corps was raised in Halifax and Huddersfield in 1798 but was disbanded in 1802. A year later it became the West Yorkshire Yeomanry Cavalry but ceased to exist seven years later. Re-raised twice in 1817 and 1843 it was eventually disbanded in 1894.

YORKSHIRE (EAST RIDING)

The East Riding Yeomanry

A regiment of three troops was raised in the East Riding of Yorkshire and existed from May 1794 until 1814. After the South African war a new regiment was accepted and was called the East Riding of Yorkshire Imperial Yeomanry: it later became a Lancer regiment, and was known as Lord Wenlock's Horse.

In 1915 the East Riding Yeomanry sailed for Macedonia, but the destination was altered and in November it landed in Egypt. It became part of the Western Frontier Force, before going on to fight in Palestine. In 1918 the Regiment was dismounted and on amalgamation became 102nd (Lincolnshire and East Riding Yeomanry) Bn, The Machine Gun Corps, serving on the Western Front.

Members of the East Riding Yeomanry formed the 26th Armoured Car Company of the Tank Corps after the Great War and retained this role until 1939 when two regiments were formed. The 1st East Riding Yeomanry served in France in 1940, and took part in the assault landings in Normandy, continuing to fight for the whole of the campaign in north-west Europe. The 2nd Regiment converted to infantry as 10th Bn, The Green Howards and later 12th Bn, The Parachute Regiment. This Battalion took part in the parachute drop on D-Day and continued to fight across France.

Re-formed in 1947 as an armoured regiment, the East Riding Yeomanry was amalgamated with the Yorkshire Dragoons and Hussars in 1956, forming the Queen's Own Yorkshire Yeomanry (qv under Yorkshire Hussars).

A patrol of the East Riding Yeomanry in Palestine, painted by J. P. Beadle.

– The Queen's Own Yorkshire Yeomanry

YORKSHIRE (NORTH RIDING)

In 1794 four troops of Yeomanry Cavalry are recorded as having been raised in the North Riding, and they served until 1802. In 1803 six troops were formed, four of which were regimented as the Richmond Forresters in 1818. In 1831 they became the York North Riding Yeomanry Cavalry and served until disbandment in 1838.

IRELAND

The History of the Irish Corps of Yeomanry during the times of the Revolutionary and Napoleonic wars is particularly difficult to trace. They were formed under separate legislation from that which governed the Yeomanry Cavalry in England, Scotland and Wales. Although a large number of corps was raised in many parts of Ireland, their fortunes varied and none has survived to modern times. For these reasons they have been excluded from this work.

A number of companies of Imperial Yeomanry were formed in Ireland for the South African war, six for various battalions and a complete battalion, the 29th Battalion, of five companies. Veterans of the South African war and other volunteers were formed into two new regiments of Imperial Yeomanry in 1902,

Trooper Cochrane of the North Irish Horse c1910.

– Colonel I. B. Gailey

A rare photograph of a member of the South Irish Horse of unknown date.

– Colonel I. B. Gailey

the North of Ireland Imperial Yeomanry and South of Ireland Imperial Yeomanry. The Territorial Force did not extend to Ireland; thus in 1908 the regiments were transferred to the Special Reserve (SR) and redesignated as below. They took precedence after the Regular Cavalry and before the Yeomanry regiments.

The North Irish Horse

The North Irish Horse was formed with four, later five, squadrons. On mobilisation, individual squadrons moved to France as divisional cavalry squadrons, starting in August 1914. In 1916 the squadrons were regrouped to form two regiments, the 1st and 2nd North Irish Horse. Both units served as corps cavalry regiments until mid-1917, when 2nd NIH was converted to infantry and absorbed into 9th Bn, the Royal Irish Fusiliers, which was given the subsidiary designation 'North Irish Horse'. The 1st NIH was converted to a cyclist battalion in March 1918 and served as such until the end of the war.

The North Irish Horse, in common with many other Special Reserve regiments (designated 'Militia' in 1921), were held in 'suspended animation' between the wars. In 1939 it was transferred from the Militia to the Supplementary Reserve and reconstituted in the Royal Armoured Corps.

In 1939 the North Irish Horse was raised again as an armoured car regiment and in 1941 converted to Valentine tanks. On moving to Tunisia in January 1943, the regiment received Churchill tanks and fought in a number of engagements during the next fifteen months. From April 1944 the regiment fought in the Italian campaign for the last year of the war.

The Territorial Army was extended to Northern Ireland in 1947 and the North Irish Horse again transferred, this time from the Supplementary Reserve to the Territorial Army, but remaining in the RAC. Two squadrons were retained in 1967. D (North Irish Horse) Squadron served with the Royal Yeomanry, but is now independent, the other serves as 69 (North Irish Horse) Signal Squadron (V). An element of the Band still exists and serves with the North Irish Staff Band.

The South Irish Horse

Six squadrons of the South Irish Horse served in the First World War. On mobilisation individual squadrons joined divisions as divisional cavalry and moved to France. In May 1916 the squadrons were grouped into two corps cavalry regiments known as 1st and 2nd South Irish Horse. The two regiments were dismounted in August 1917, amalgamated, and converted to infantry to form 7th (South Irish Horse) Bn, the Royal Irish Regiment, under which designation they served for the rest of the war. The Battalion sustained heavy casualties at St Quentin in March 1918 and fought at the Battle of Courtrai in October.

In common with other units originating in the South of Ireland, the South Irish Horse were disbanded following Partition in 1922.

OTHER COUNTIES

There are no records of Yeomanry serving at any time in the following counties – Banffshire, Kincardineshire, Merionethshire and Radnorshire.

A troop from Brecknockshire served for a time in the Montgomeryshire Yeomanry, and there is evidence of a Yeomanry Cavalry corps in Bute.

The two Highland regiments drew recruits from the following counties at various times: The Scottish Horse – Aberdeenshire, Argyllshire, Morayshire and Nairnshire; The Lovat Scouts – Aberdeenshire, Caithness, Orkney, Outer Hebrides (Skye and South Uist Squadron), Ross and Cromarty, Shetland and Sutherland.

First Aid Nursing Yeomanry

An unofficial corps was formed in London in 1907 called the First Aid Nursing Yeomanry (FANY). Comprised of public-spirited ladies of gentle birth, they envisaged a requirement for a service to render medical treatment to mounted troops. Official (but unfunded) recognition was given in 1927, although many individual members contrived to serve in France in the Great War, as ambulance drivers and nurses.

In 1937 the FANY became part of the Women's Transport Service and there were contingents in India and Kenya, as well as in Britain. Three members won the George Cross for their part in special operations in occupied countries during the Second World War. The FANY continues in being to the present day with a communications role.

Select Bibliography

NARRATIVE SECTION

ANGLESEY, Marquess of *History of the British Cavalry 1816–1919*, Volumes I, II and III, London, Leo Cooper 1973–82.

FORTESCUE, Hon. J. W. *History of the British Army 1783–1803*, London, Macmillan, 1908.

FREEMAN, Benson F. M. *The Yeomanry of Devon 1794–1927*, London, St Catherine's Press, 1927.

MILEHAM, P. J. R. *The Stirlingshire Yeomanry Cavalry and the Scottish Insurrection of 1820*, Journal of the Society for Army Historical Research, Volume LXIII 1985.
The Yeomanry – A Short History, Shalford, The Yeomanry Association, 1983.

SEBAG-MONTEFIORE, C. *History of the Volunteer Forces*, London, Constable 1908.

TEICHMAN, Major O. *Yeomanry at Gallipoli, Rafa, Gaza I, II and III, Balin and El Mughar.* Series of articles in the Cavalry Journal, 1934–7.
Yeomanry as an Aid to Civil Power, Journal of the Society for Army Historical Research Vol XIX, 1940.

(See also WHITE, A. S. under Regimental Section, for Yeomanry regimental histories.)

REGIMENTAL SECTION

FREDERICK, J. B. M. *Lineage Book of the British Army, Mounted Corps and Infantry 1660–1969*, New York, Hope Farm Press, 1969.

FREEMAN, Benson F. M. and **FELLOWS**, G. *Historical Records of the South Notts Hussars*, Aldershot, Gale and Polden, 1928.

JAMES, Brigadier E. A. *British Regiments 1914–18*, London, Samson, 1978.

JOSLEN, Lieut Col H. F. *Orders of Battle 1939–1945*, Volumes I and II, London, Her Majesty's Stationery Office, 1960.

MARTIN, Colonel A. R. *Lineage Charts of the Yeomanry and Infantry of the Territorial Army* – unpublished.

OFFICIAL PUBLICATIONS *The Army List*, (various dates).
Army Orders 1920–22.
Revised Titles and Designations of Major Units of the Territorial Army 1951.
Army Orders and Defence Council Instructions, 1967 onwards.
Territorial and Army Volunteer Reserve Units and sub-unit titles, 1976 onwards.

SLEIGH, A. *Royal Militia and Yeomanry Cavalry List*, London, British Army Despatch Press, 1850

ROYAL ARTILLERY INSTITUTION. *Royal Artillery Commemoration Book, 1939–1945*, London, 1950.

RICHARDS, W. *His Majesty's Territorial Army*, London, J. S. Virtue, 1908.

WHITE, A. S. *Bibliography of Regimental Histories of the British Army*, London, Society for Army Historical Research and Army Museums, Ogilby Trust, 1965.

SPECIALIST SUBJECTS

BAKER, H. *The Territorial Force. A Manual of its law, organisation and administration* (Foreword by Rt Hon R. B. Haldane), London, John Murray, 1909.

BARLOW, L. and **SMITH**, R. J. *Uniforms of the British Yeomanry Forces 1794–1914*. Series of booklets, Robert Ogilby Trust, from 1979.

CARMAN, W. Y. *Head-dresses of the British Army – Yeomanry*, Sutton, W. Y. Carman, 1970.

EDWARDS, Major T. J. *Regimental Badges* (revised A. L. Kipling), three editions, Aldershot, Gale and Polden 1950, 1956, 1965.

HARRIS, R. G. *Fifty years of Yeomanry Uniforms*, London, Frederick Muller, 1972.

ROBSON, B. *Swords of the British Army – The Regulation Patterns 1788–1914*, London, Arms and Armour Press, 1975.

SAINSBURY, J. D. *Hertfordshire Yeomanry and Artillery Uniforms, Arms and Equipment, Volume I.*, Herts Yeomanry Historical Trust, 1980.

SIMKIN, R. *British Yeomanry Uniforms*, (Introductory Notes by L. V. Archer), London, Frederick Muller, 1972.

SMITHERMAN, P. H. *Uniforms of the Yeomanry Regiments 1783–1911*, London, Hugh Evelyn 1967.

TYLDEN, G. *Horses and Saddlery*, London, J. A. Allen/Army Museums, Ogilby Trust, 1965. *The use of Firearms by Cavalry*, Journal of the Society for Army Historical Research, Volume XIX, 1940.

WILKINSON, F. *Cavalry and Yeomanry badges of the British Army 1914*, London, Arms and Armour Press 1973.

Acknowledgements

The Author acknowledges with gratitude the following individuals, institutions, museums and museum trusts, who supplied or assisted in the illustrations, photographs and written material.

J. Anderson Esq
G. Archer Parfitt Esq
Major J. D. Bastin
Major D. S. Barrington-Browne
Colonel J. H. Boag OBE MC TD DL
Colonel D. S. Casstles TD DL
Lt Col R. M. T. Campbell-Preston OBE MC TD DL
Lt Col P. T. Champness OBE TD
Colonel G. V. Churton MBE MC TD DL
Colonel R. D. N. Fabricius CBE TD JP
Major J. H. Gardner MBE TD JP
Colonel I. B. Gailey TD
Major R. J. B. Gentry TD
Colonel Sir John Gilmour Bart, DSO TD JP
Major A. G. Harfield
R. Hasell McCosh Esq
Major R. M. Heelis
Colonel W. P. Howells OBE TD DL
Colonel J. W. Isaacs MBE TD
Revd J. M. James
Capt S. W. Ledger
Major D. D. A. Linaker
Major D. H. Manders TD
Colonel P. J. D. McCraith MC TD DL
Major B. Mollo TD
Colonel P. S. Newton MBE
Lt Col G. W. A. Norton
Lt Col J. G. Peel TD
Colonel H. C. B. Rogers OBE
D. Ross Esq
Major B. O. Simmonds
Major M. T. Steiger
Major J. M. A. Tamplin TD
Colonel G. D. Thompson MC TD DL
J. Tyler Esq
Colonel E. C. York TD ADC
Major J. C. K. Young

Army Museums' Ogilby Trust
Ayrshire Yeomanry
Bedfordshire Yeomanry
Berkshire Yeomanry
Carmarthenshire Antiquarian Society
Central Office of Information
Cheshire Yeomanry
Royal Devon Yeomanry
Essex Yeomanry
Directorate of Army Recruiting
Directorate of Public Relations (Army)
Duke of Lancaster's Own Yeomanry
Dyfed County Council
Royal Gloucestershire Hussars
Royal Green Jackets, Oxford
Hertfordshire Yeomanry
Imperial War Museum
Inns of Court and City Yeomanry
Leicestershire and Derbyshire Yeomanry
Logistic Executive (Army)
Lovat Scouts
Kent and Sharpshooters Yeomanry
Middlesex Yeomanry
National Army Museum
Northumberland Hussars
Pembroke Yeomanry
Powysland Museum
Royal Artillery Institution
Scottish Horse
Sherwood Rangers Yeomanry
Shropshire Yeomanry
South Notts Hussars
Staff College, Camberley
Staffordshire Yeomanry
Suffolk and Norfolk Yeomanry
Surrey Yeomanry
Sussex Yeomanry
The Tank Museum
Wellington College
Westminster Dragoons
Royal Wiltshire Yeomanry
Worcestershire Yeomanry
Worcester City Museum and Art Gallery
The Queen's Own Yorkshire Yeomanry

Index

Individual troops and former names of regiments of Yeomanry Cavalry are not indexed.

Sherman tanks of 2nd Fife & Forfar Yeomanry at Bayeux, June 1944